MINIVAN MOGUL

A CRASH COURSE IN CONFIDENCE FOR WOMEN

BY ALEX PERRY

Copyright © 2020 by Alexandra Perry

ISBN: 978-1-7341262-8-0 (hard cover)
      978-1-7350915-3-2 (soft cover)

Edited by: Karli Jackson, Monika Dziamka, and Amy Ashby

Warren publishing

Published by Warren Publishing
Charlotte, NC
www.warrenpublishing.net
Printed in the United States

For my beautiful daughter, Carmen,
may the road to confidence always be clear for you.

CONTENTS

ACKNOWLEDGMENTS

L ife isn't meant be done alone, and no good work is done in isolation. It's taken more than a metropolis to get this book into the world, and "thank you" seems like an insufficient way to express the gratitude I feel for everyone who has stepped up and encouraged me along the way.

To my daughter, Carmen: In the fourteen short years of your life, you have taught me more about confidence than all of my other efforts combined. You are my inspiration, forever my joy, and without a doubt, my reason for breathing. You have made me a stronger person in every way, and being your mom will always be my greatest accomplishment in life. I love you more than words can say.

To my husband, Clark: You are my toughest critic and my biggest champion. A compliment earned from you means more than a thousand from others. You've stood by me, comforted me, pushed me, and cheered me through every crazy endeavor I've taken on. Through every job change, every long run, while launching the business, and all other ups and downs life has brought us, you've been there, steady as ever—many times carrying the bags (literally, the gear bags), and without taking the credit you deserve for providing the stability to allow me to pursue my dreams. I couldn't ask for a better friend and partner in life than you. I love you.

To my stepkiddos Kayla and Phillip: Oh boy, we have some road trip memories, don't we? Our journey together hasn't always been smooth; however, I wouldn't change it. You've taught me more about patience, grace, and love than anyone else. Phillip, your endless curiosity and questions inspire me to think more broadly and intently about the world. I blame you in the best possible way for my political interests and growth. Thank you for being the son that I didn't get to have on my own. Thank you for letting me come to your games and cheer for you. Thanks for loving the food I make and for making me laugh. I wanted a boy so badly, and God gave me you. Thank you for asking about the book all along the way and for encouraging me to finish it. Kayla, thank you for letting me love you like I do. Your generosity of spirit, your ability to always be thinking of others, and willingness to give without expectation of return are just a few of the ways I try to emulate you. You are a gift to those who are blessed to know you. I love being your stepmom; I love calling you mine. I love you, period.

To my sister, Charlotte: Thank you for being the role model I needed throughout my entire life. You've been more than a sister; you've been my mom, my best friend, my therapist, and my partner in shenanigans. You are my favorite person to road trip with (even if you eat apples and I eat Cheetos) because the conversations go around and around in a thousand beautiful ways and never truly end. I wouldn't be where I am today had it not been for you. You took me in, made sure I stayed the course, and have kept track of me ever since. You get me, and I love you so much it hurts.

To my brother-in-law, Doug: I didn't want you to think I forgot you in my effusiveness about Charlotte. I appreciate you being you, for telling me GO DO IT and for editing endless amounts a blogposts for me. It takes a village to take care of me, and I'm grateful you're my family.

To Adrian and Cara: Thank you for being the best brother- and sister-in-law a woman could ask for. You get me. You encourage me, and you make me laugh. Adrian, you make fun of me, but deep down, I know how proud you are of me, and I want you to know how proud I am of you.

To Claire, my beautiful, quirky, funny niece: Don't let the world stop you from being you. The world needs you as you are. You inspire me always to embrace creativity.

To my parents: Dad, you taught me the value of listening to others and the power of not adding commentary. You encouraged me to read and to read aloud, both skills that have profoundly changed me as a person. Thank you for letting me be me. Mom, you've been an endless cheerleader as I've ventured out on my own. My love of all things quirky, funny, and pun-y comes from you. To Phil and Barbara, thank you both for being the partners my parents needed and for loving me even though I wasn't "your own."

To Jenni Robbins: I blame you in the best possible way for all of this. You have been whispering in my ear since the beginning, reminding me to be myself, encouraging me to be better, and listening to all of my secrets. You are a mogul maker, and my life has been forever changed by having met you.

To all of the women of the Badass Women's Council: I friggin' love you. Rebecca, Jenni, Lindsay, Nicole, Erin, and Emily, you've inspired me, loved me, cried with me, laughed with me, and pushed me to be the best possible version of myself. I'm grateful to be on the road of life with you. You will always have a reserved seat in the minivan.

To Rebecca: We go all the way back to gymnastics days with our girls; who would've ever dreamed we'd both be writing books, owning our own businesses, and partnering with each other to make this world a better place? I'm grateful for your mentorship, your friendship, and your crazy sense of humor.

To Jason, my brother from another mother: Thank you for listening to all my "whatifabouts." Thank you for praying with me, praying for me, and standing beside me no matter what. Your fire inspires me daily, and I'm blessed to call you my friend.

To Jess and "Maybe Andy" and the Craig kids: Thank you for your friendship. For Marvel Comic-movie watching. For laughing and dreaming and CrossFit-ing.

To Darcy and her book club (Leah, Christine, Lila, and Katie): Thank you for reading the book before it was ever fit to see the light of day. Thank you for pouring in your thoughts, your encouragement, and your sage advice. This book is better because of you.

To Mikelle: You didn't even know me, but you were willing to read my book in its early stages and give me advice that made a huge difference in its evolution. It's a pretty wild thing to read a book for someone who you don't know and then give constructive feedback, and you did it well. Thank you for hopping in for the ride.

To Annie: It's a special friend who allows a story about her poop problems to be put into print. You're just that kind of special. You have made me a better person, a better momma, and a better coach. Thank you for allowing me to pour into your life and for pouring into mine. I love you.

To Ricki: I can't remember what life was like before you. You infiltrated my life (or did I infiltrate yours?) and we've been inseparable ever since. Even a move to another state hasn't kept us far apart. You were one of the first to know about my dream of having a business, my dream of coaching, and then the dream of this book. Not once did you ever discourage me. You gave me room to dream and encouragement to go on, even when it was tough. Part sister, part daughter, forever friend. You are one of a very few ride-or-dies in my life, and I love you more than you know.

To Amy Kincaid: Thank you for being a supporter from the start and for always reminding me that not everyone knows the "big words" I'm using. You keep me real. Love you.

To Jen Edds, the friend I desperately wished I'd had in eighth grade: Thank you for the endless Voxer chats, for listening to my fears, and for telling me my minivan is cool. You literally make me sound better in videos, on my upcoming podcast, and in my talks. I am so grateful the Universe brought us together. We were meant to be. Like Beavis and Butthead.

To Karli Jackson and Monika Dziamka for your editing eyes and gracious hearts. You've done the hard part of polishing this book, and I'm beyond grateful for your time and energy.

To Mindy Kuhn and Amy Ashby of Warren Publishing for saying "yes," walking me through the process, and believing in my minivan ways.

To Tony and Jen (a.k.a. the other half of the parental council): I can't imagine life without both of you. Thank you for being the parental support I need, every time I need it. Thank you for co-parenting and co-loving our kids. Thank you for sharing Katie and Colin with me, I am blessed to be their "Miss Alex." Thank you for embracing a non-traditional life that has brought more love, laughter, and support than we could've ever dreamed at the start. What we have was never part of the plan, but every great story has a plot twist and ours has been the best kind ever. Jen, thank you for supporting and encouraging my business from day one. Practically Speaking wouldn't be what it is were it not for you encouraging me to go for it. Tony, thank you for loving Carmen fiercely and for never her letting go.

To Bryn Jafri and my Three Kings Athletics family: Thank you for making me a stronger person, mentally and physically. Our gym is my home away from home and you are a part of family.

To my friends who are mentioned in the pages that follow: Mike Bensi, Joshua Bach, Harrison Painter, and Steven Vrooman. Thank you for being a part of my story.

I don't know when to stop! When do you stop saying thank you? I could thank EVERYBODY. I mean EVERYBODY. This book was not created in a vacuum, at all. If by some gross error I didn't include your name here, please insert it (I've included a line here for you below), because I appreciate you. I appreciate you holding this book in your hands right now.

Thank you, _____.

FOREWORD

There's no one I'd rather climb in a minivan with than Alex Perry. Not necessarily because she's the best driver! She has the best snacks, and she'll smile and laugh and make the trip fun and meaningful. Alex has taken her journey with all the ups and downs and said, "Hey, jump in, let me take you for a ride around the block of confidence." I wouldn't tell you to jump in a van with just anyone—that's creepy—but this one? Yeah, jump in, you bring the Cheetos; she'll bring the stories.

I've ridden along with Alex on this "confidence" journey. She's been ridiculously intentional with allowing herself to feel "all the things" along the way. She's stood in the suck of discomfort and asked what it was meant to teach her. She's stood on the stage and received the applause and thanked those around her.

All the while, she's remained unapologetically Alex. This is her superpower. As you read these incredibly helpful and meaningful lessons in courage, you'll derive great benefit, not because Alex is perfect or the expert, but because she's willing to share her story. When we stand tall in our stories, we encourage others to do the same. Alex's invitation for me to jump in the minivan with her says everything about her and this book. In these pages, she's inviting you to be you. And she's willing to drive and let you ride along, sharing her story with humor, vulnerability, and deeply meaningful experiences.

These are the stories we crave as everyday women. I get so excited thinking of the amazing power when the everyday woman, loaded with laughter and more confidence, takes to the streets after reading this book. Be ready—the minivan moguls are hitting the streets in big ways.

Rebecca Fleetwood Hession,
CEO AND FOUNDER OF BADASS WOMEN'S COUNCIL, AUTHOR

INTRODUCTION

*G*ot confidence problems?

I thought you might. That's why you picked up this book—because you're looking for a way to feel confident. You want to be confident about yourself, exactly as you are. I hear you, my newfound friend.

Trying to be a confident woman in today's world is tough. Brutal, actually. The world around us is constantly handing us opportunities to feel like poo—to question everything about ourselves and, therefore, rattling our confidence every single day. I mean, think about it: when was the last time you got on social media and thought, "Man, that really helped me feel better about myself. There's nothing like seeing how much better everyone else is doing to give a gal the confidence she needs to face the day."

Give me a break. It's a good day if you can get up and walk past the mirror and *not* mutter "ugh" while you pinch, lift, or suck something in. We are bombarded—now more than ever before—by the media, with images and stories of what we should look like, how we should act, how we should speak, and all the things we should have if we are going to be confident in ourselves.

If you're like me, you see images of people who appear to be nailing it, hustling their way to success: rock stars, influencers, mother-of-the-year types, boss babes. And you wonder, "Is that what I'm supposed to be doing? Are these people for real? What if I don't want to hustle? What if I never 'make it'? Does that mean I'm somehow less than the other people in my life, people on social media, or in the news?" You're struggling because at some point along the way you've bought into the idea that somewhere out there is a checklist of traits, possessions, or accomplishments you must have before you can feel, before you can even say the words: *"I am confident."*

You've probably tried to change, hide, or cover up parts of yourself as a way to manufacture confidence. You've sought value through and in other people, like your boss, your family, or your friends by bending yourself to fit their ideas of the best, most successful version of you. You've spent a lot of time and worked hard to be good at *everything*. A good employee, a good wife, a good mom, a good friend. Because, if you're really good at it all, you'll feel—you'll *be*—confident. You've bought all. the. things. The clothes, the jewelry, the makeup, the house, the car ... you name it, because status symbols are supposed to help you feel more confident, right?

You've made Pinterest boards for the house and waxed your eyebrows into oblivion. You've read book after book after book. You've watched a thousand videos in an effort to motivate yourself toward confidence, and you beat yourself up afterward because you spent part of that time watching funny dog videos.

You've tried changing darn near everything about yourself, but it hasn't worked, has it? Talk about a confidence drain suck. It's a tough world out there, my friend. And at the end of the day, after all your efforts, you still struggle with your confidence, and it's led you down a road of frustration and anxiety and questioning the universe about whether or not you're ever going to figure out a way to feel confident just as you are, where you are, right now.

That's why you're here reading this book. I get it—I know what it's like to struggle with confidence. I know what it feels like to be struggling just to get through the day. I don't have thousands of social media followers, a nanny, or a personal chef. I drive a 2014 Toyota Sienna minivan that's questionably clean most of the time, and by that, I mean *not* clean. There's for sure an old Cheeto under the seat, dog slobber on the windows, and sand from last year's vacation in the back. I know more about the struggles you face every day as an everyday woman than a social media celebrity does any day of the week. I know the struggle to feel confident in my work when it seems like the rest of the world has it all put together. I understand what it's like to be awkward and weird and to really mess stuff up. I've felt deep longing to quit trying and live as a hermit in my basement, subsisting on Cheetos and Netflix.

I have struggled, and I can now admit *with confidence* that I still have days when I struggle with being true to myself. Isn't it time we start admitting that to ourselves and to each other? *Minivan Mogul.* You probably laughed when you read it. It makes me laugh too. Moguls don't drive minivans, right? I'm not a mogul in the traditional sense—I am an average, everyday woman just like you. I am a hardworking, minivan-driving mom. I am not a social-media mogul, a celebrity mogul, or a business mogul. I am a *minivan mogul*—an important person to my family, my friends, my clients, and, most notably, to myself. And in my world, that's more important than being a mogul by anyone else's standards. It's been because of my struggles, not despite them, that I've learned a few key lessons that have helped me feel confident where I am, as I am, regardless of my current circumstances. They're lessons I have to remind myself of every single day. They're the lessons that help me remain confident in who I am, and that's why I want to share them with you. That's why I decided to write this book.

If you're struggling with confidence, you've come to the right place. I'm with you on the confidence struggle bus (or in the struggle minivan), and I'm here to help. I'm here to serve as a guide to help you find your way to your truest self, and as with any trip that starts off with two strangers, by the end we'll know each other quite well, and I hope we'll consider ourselves good friends. Woman, I'm here to tell you, you are in the driver's seat when it comes to being confident, and it's time you take control. You, my friend, can be the confident woman you're meant to be.

This is a crash course in confidence. We've got no time to waste. I've written this book while keeping in mind that you are an incredibly busy woman. You don't have time for deep, philosophical conversations on confidence. You need help right here, right now. You need advice that's straightforward and accessible. In this book, I've provided for you short, impactful, and oftentimes funny stories that can be read in your minivan, in the car-rider line, or while you wait to check out at Target. Many of these stories were scribbled on bits of notepaper, odd receipts, or a wrapper in my own minivan.

They're stories I processed behind the wheel as I drove to and from appointments, to the store, or to take my kiddo, Carmen, to and from activities. To be honest, I used to be embarrassed by my van. I used to think, *Someday I'll buy myself a fancy car.* I used to think, *CEOs don't drive minivans.* Not anymore. *I am a minivan-driving mom* from the Midwest who has navigated all kinds of twists and turns on this road called life. I started my own company where I've been lucky enough to meet and coach young graduates, CEOs, TEDx speakers, aspiring speakers, and all kinds of people in between. I've volunteered at school events, served as a church group leader, and made cookies for the neighbors. I've traveled across the country to deliver keynotes and lead corporate workshops and group trainings. I work out a lot and am unashamed to say that sometimes I do it just so I can eat Cheetos. I've been published in *Forbes,* and in March 2019, I gave my first TEDx talk. And now I've written this book—something that I hadn't planned on and didn't think I could do. It's funny how life works that way—no matter how much we plan, we just don't quite know where the road of life will take us.

This book highlights the lessons, or "road rules" as I call them, that I've learned about being confident. They're designed to help you feel confident with who you are, where you are, right now. You can think of them as a sort of internal GPS—a guidance system to help you be your truest self with a little less frustration and confusion.

As you continue to read, you're going to want to have a pen and paper handy (or a candy wrapper will work too) because at the end of each section, you'll have the chance to reflect on the lessons and answer a few questions to help you apply them to your own life.

It is my hope that by me sharing these stories with you, you'll find confidence in yourself no matter your circumstances. I hope you'll find joy, peace, and the kind of success you're looking for by being confident in yourself. I hope you'll then take what you've learned and share it with someone else to make that person's journey a little easier.

OK, it's time to buckle up, settle in, and enjoy the ride. As you read, picture yourself sitting next to me in my minivan, telling you these stories. There's music in the background, bags of Cheetos to snack on, and cold drinks in the cup holders. We'll laugh, we'll cry, and there will be moments when we turn the radio down, not knowing what to say, and we'll sit in silence to think. We'll be confident together.

P.S.
A minivan trumps a Maserati every time.
Why? Because there's always room for more people in a van.

CHAPTER ONE

ROAD RULE 1: WHEN IN DOUBT, STEER TOWARD CONFIDENCE.

*"I used to have this philosophy of
'fake it till you make it.' And now, I just own it."*

—JUDALINE CASSIDY, TRADESWOMAN,
PIONEERING UNION MEMBER, TEACHER, PLUMBER[1]

Introduction

The problem you continue to have with confidence is that you're trying to find it, buy it, or get it from someone else. You might feel like you don't have what it takes or that you don't have everything you need to be confident. Despite what you might see and read on social media, you don't need a different job, a side hustle, or more likes, clicks, and followers to have confidence. You don't need a special outfit, more knowledge, a fancy car, or a bigger house to have it. You don't need the perfect a.m. routine, rock-hard abs, or a perfectly organic diet to have it. You don't need to wait for your boss, your family, or your friends to say the perfect words of encouragement that will magically bestow confidence upon you. That's never going to happen.

Ultimately, no matter how many gurus you read or watch, not a single of one them can give you confidence. Other people can only point the way. Confidence isn't something to be built, found, purchased, or given. It's not something you've got to develop, and it's not something you have to build up to. You don't need more experience to have it. You already carry confidence deep within you. You see, you already have everything you need to be confident, and all you have to do is make the choice to be confident. Like choosing which turn to take or road to drive down, you get to choose whether or not you're confident in yourself.

You probably don't remember this, but you were born confident. Until the world got to you, you wore confidence like it was your job. Think back for a moment: I bet when you were little, you ran around in your own confident-kid bliss doing all the things you loved to do. Maybe you were the kid who wore cowboy boots and a Spiderman shirt everywhere, including church, the mall, and Grandma's house. Or maybe you were the kid who stood on the street corner, singing and dancing at the top of your lungs with your friends, knowing *for a fact* that there would be a music agent who would *for sure* be driving through your neighborhood, and that you'd be discovered and whisked away to Hollywood. Or maybe you were the kid who sat in the corner with the Crayola crayon super pack—you remember, the one with the sharpener—and a pad of paper, drawing endless pictures, knowing that each one was a masterpiece, ultimately priceless because they were made by you. Remember that kid? That kid was confident. *You* were confident.

And then somewhere along the way, you became aware of what everyone else thought about what you were doing. The annoying kid in second grade made fun of your Spiderman T-shirt, so ... you put it away. The old neighbor lady looked at you and told you to "cut it out, don't you know you can't sing?" Or you handed your perfect picture, the one of the horse you spent hours drawing, to your mom and she said, "Oh, what is that? A dog? That's nice, dear ...." That was the day you became aware of what others think, and your confidence shrunk.

Flash forward to now, and you've experienced confidence blows left and right. Rejection, criticism, and judgment from strangers, from friends, from family, from coworkers. You've taken in their comments, and you hold them as your truth.

"Everyone tells me I'm picky."

"I'm just a hot mess—I can't get organized."

"I'm so dumb—I can't figure this stuff out on my own."

"I'm not good enough, smart enough, fast enough, talented enough."

And on, and on, and on. With each thought, you choose not to be confident—you choose what someone else says about you over your own confidence in who you are. And that's a mistake.

You're not alone. I've been there too, and it's caused a lot of pain for me—pain that I'd love to help you avoid. Choosing confidence is a lesson I wish I'd learned sooner. It's a lesson I have to practice daily. There have been many times when I've looked for confidence everywhere, but where I needed to look for it the most was within myself. I let others define who I am, rather than having confidence in myself and my abilities. I looked externally for confidence, which wasn't ever going to get me there. As we move on, the stories that follow will illustrate how to steer yourself toward confidence. Settle in and enjoy the ride.

P.S.
You are in the driver's seat.
Steer toward confidence.

"Being anything other than confident seems like a lot of work."

–Carmen Rufatto, Teenager, Lover of Music, Confidence Prodigy

My daughter, Carmen, is wise. We were talking one day about *confidence*. She has sailed through life so far, feeling good about who she is and what she does. Let me give you a couple of examples.

When she was three, I gave her crackers and cheese slices. She placed a slice of cheese on top of a cracker, held it up, and exclaimed, "I a child genius!" (The irony of her statement was *not* lost on us.)

At eight, I offered her dance lessons. She told me, "I don't need lessons, Momma; I already *know* how to dance."

At eleven, she told us that if she "had a source of income and access to transportation" she would no longer need parents. *Tempting.*

Confidence is her game.

I asked her, "Baby, why are you so confident?"

She thought about it for half a second and said, "Being anything other than confident seems like a lot of work, and I don't want to do that much work."

My dear reader, let that statement sink in. What if we're making confidence much harder than it has to be? What if what's actually hard *isn't* being confident—it's the other way around? What if we considered doubt, worry, and feeling insecure as *hard work*, and we viewed confidence as *easy* and *natural*?

What would happen? How would your life change if you chose confidence?

P.S.

People ask me all the time if Carmen really is this confident.
I can tell you with absolute confidence—ha!—that she is.
The lesson here? When we as moms, as women, are
confident around each other, it rubs off. Choose to be
confident around those whom you care about.

Confidence doesn't come in a syringe

"Embedded in the everyday is a magnificence that is so easy to miss because we're so mired in the struggle and what society says we are."

—Ava Duvernay, Entertainment PR Firm Owner,
Film Producer and Distributor, Midlife Career Changer[2]

Can we talk about being confident when it comes to our looks? I don't know what life has been like for you in relation to your appearance, but I can tell you that for me, trying to be confident about how I look has been a struggle since puberty and has continued throughout my life. The only difference between the negative self-images I fought back in my teen years and the ones I fight now is that I can now find more reasons to be negative about how I look than I could back then.

Time marches on, so they say, but they should probably add that it marches all over your face too. Wrinkles, drooping skin, a belly that was never tight but is now even less so, veins, weird-looking age spots—that's what time brings. Thank you, time ... thanks a lot. Now, don't get me wrong, I'm not an overly vain person. I believe that each person has a unique beauty about them, no matter the age, hair color, ethnicity, etc. It's just a heck of a lot easier to find that beauty in other people than it is to find it in myself.

I live, and chances are that you do too, in America, where the beauty standards are insane, to say the least. Retouched photos of women with thigh gaps, perfect noses, flawless skin, long, long legs, and perfectly toned tushes are splattered all over the internet, magazines, and commercials, often with the mixed message of attaining *real* beauty. Give me a break. The intoxicating promises of creams, shots, makeup, lotions, potions, and weird infomercials all claim that if we just do a little more, we'll be more beautiful—and we'll feel that way too. What a load of crap. If that were true,

I would've felt good about my skin back in '84 when I sat on my bedroom floor, coated in an entire pot of Noxzema cream. *Sigh.* I heard once that if women decided to stop buying beauty care products, we would bring the American economy to a screeching halt. Wouldn't that be something?

Being confident about our appearances is challenging, to say the least, and in a world of instant gratification, it becomes exceptionally hard not to buy into the idea that if we just do a little more, we'll feel good about how we look. Let me give you an example from the not-too-recent past.

I went to the dermatologist because, as I've aged, I've developed these super-cute things on my face called overactive sebaceous glands. Super-cute is said here with heavy sarcasm. Basically, some of the oil glands in my face have malfunctioned, leaving me with tiny bumps all over, as well as what I'll call a nice, healthy glow (i.e., my face looks like an oil slick most of the time). The dermatologist told me there are some things that I could do to help tame the little beasts and suggested I talk with an aesthetician about possible treatments.

Let's pause here for a moment: I've avoided aestheticians for my entire adult life because I don't want to be sold on stuff that I don't need. I got a facial once and ended up with a seventy-five-dollar bottle of cream that did nothing for me other than make my pocketbook hurt. If you're an aesthetician or the type of person who loves going to see these types of folks, please don't take this personally—this really isn't about skin-care professionals or your love of facials. I promise. I just try to be a practical person (remember, I proudly drive a minivan), and I don't want a bunch of powders and potions and treatments for my face. I'm also a realist. Time is marching across my face and I know it. I want to handle that fact with as much grace as I can.

Anyway, I decided it might be worth my time and effort to go ahead and see someone because, while being practical and a realist,

I still want to look as good as I possibly can, and the dumb bumps on my face annoy me.

I went in prepared for the appointment. Valerie was the aesthetician's name, and she was very kind. I wanted to be sure she knew what I was there for. I told her I wasn't interested in learning about products for anything other than the overly excited glands on my face, and I made sure to say, *"Please don't try to sell me Botox; I'm not interested."*

Let's pause here again, because I recognize that I could be treading on dangerous ground here with you. Lots and lots of folks, including many of my friends, are Botox fans. I think that's great. If you get Botox and it makes you feel positive about how you look, then more power to you. It isn't my place to tell you what to do with your face. I'm merely relaying my experience and preferences here as a way to highlight one way of thinking positively about yourself. One way—not the only way. OK, let's resume.

When I told Valerie right off the bat that I wasn't interested in Botox, she immediately said, "Are you *sure* you don't want some Botox? I mean, we live in a world of instant gratification, ya know? This will give it to ya."

I thought, *You've got to be kidding me.* Valerie clearly uses Botox—her eyebrows didn't move at all as she tried to give me a sort of knowing glance. She even said something about how we were the same age. This was not helpful in my case because I would've pegged her as much older. I'm in the camp that says the more of that stuff you use, the older and less happy you look. Our eyes were designed to smile, not to stay frozen in place.

I mean, I get it, she's paid to sell stuff, and honestly, if she'd been referring to Cheetos, I would've been all in. But some sort of toxic substance that immobilizes my muscles? Not so much. I don't want it, I don't need it, and I'm honestly worried about how it's being touted to women—even really young women—as a permanent solution to the "problem" of aging. I politely declined the Botox and told her I really wasn't interested. She said she understood, and we talked about alternative treatments for the troubles I was having. Valerie and I continue to work together to treat my face and she has, to this day, not mentioned Botox again. Thank you, Valerie. We don't have to agree on everything to be able to work together.

What Valerie said stuck with me though: *"We live in a world of instant gratification."* I don't disagree, and there's much to be said for instant gratification. I like Amazon Prime as much as the next minivan-driving mom, but like I said, I'm also a realist. The truth is, no matter how much stuff I put onto or into my face, no matter how many pounds of kale I eat, or how many crunches I do, I'm still going to be my age. *And that means the real (authentic) me is still going to peek out around the edges.* Gray hairs will shoot out, lines will continue to form, and another part of me will droop. If I'm lucky, *I'm going to grow old* ... and so are you. I mean, last time I checked, immortality is not available yet on the Kroger ClickList. I can remember complaining to a friend about turning forty—she looked right at me and told me to shut my face. She said, "Listen, my friend, there are many people who didn't make it this far. Be grateful you did." Whoa, reality check noted.

The way I'm choosing to see things now is that I've earned every line, crease, and furrow in my face. I try to look at the changes in my body, my hair, and my skin as a beautiful alternative to not being here on this planet, enjoying my friends, family, and work. Look, I know it's hard to be confident about your looks in a world that's so quick to point out our flaws, oftentimes by companies and individuals wanting to sell us something. It's hard to be confident about our bodies and faces when we're continually assaulted with the idea that we are somehow *less than* because of how we look. But isn't there so much more that makes us beautiful than just our physical appearance? Aren't you tired of chasing something that's other than who you are? Think about it for a moment—doesn't being the very best version of yourself include being confident in your own skin—wrinkled or not? You get to choose whether or not you feel beautiful, so be sure to steer yourself in the right direction.

P.S.

I shared this story with a good friend of mine who was contemplating Botox. She's an elite athlete, has seven kids, and is one of the most beautiful people I know, inside and out. She decided against the Botox, saying, *"I have a line in my forehead for each one of my kids, and I think that's beautiful."* She chose to be confident in who she is and how she looks right now.

Next time, I'm ordering the pizza

"Ambition is not a dirty word. It's believing in yourself and your abilities. What would happen if we were all brave enough to be a little ambitious? I think the world would change."

–Reese Witherspoon, Oscar Award-Winning Actor, Producer, Entrepreneur[3]

If you've ever had to meet someone you didn't know, and it didn't go as you'd hoped, this story should resonate with you. Choosing to be confident in yourself, in the choices you make, and how you interact with others can be a daunting challenge and, as in this particular instance, it's especially hard if you don't feel like things have gotten off on the right foot from the get-go. I'm guessing you're a lot like me, and you're a person who genuinely loves people. And I'm guessing that, like me, you're human and, therefore, face the challenges that many people face when they meet somone new … like making your introduction awkward, running out of questions to ask the other person, asking weird questions, talking only about yourself and then feeling bad about it, forgetting the other person's name, etc. Meeting someone new can bring out lots of our insecurities, as it did in this case for me.

A colleague was kind enough to introduce me to a woman who works in a similar field and was someone who she thought would be a beneficial contact for me as I was trying to grow my new business. I was really looking forward to the meeting. I made sure I had ready what I thought were insightful questions, and I felt pretty good as I pulled into the parking lot of the pizza place where we were meeting.

When the woman I was meeting walked in, I couldn't help but notice how she looked me up and down. We do this to people—give them the quick once-over to get a sense of who they are and how they operate. It's instinctive, this quick check-out ritual, and if you're unprepared to catch someone doing it, like I was, it can rattle your confidence. I *knew* immediately that this was not going to be the type of meeting I'd hoped for. The thing here is that I really didn't know a thing about what she was thinking of me.

You could call it a vibe, a one hundred-millisecond assessment or snap judgment of her nonverbal behavior. But in truth, it was a lack of confidence in myself based on what was, in all reality, behavior that's pretty normal from another human. When I spotted her doing it, I felt like she was sizing me up and that she had deemed me someone she'd talk to just to be nice, and that was going to be that. Now, I had *no idea* if that was true or not, but it doesn't matter—I believed it. I got it into my head that she didn't think I was up to snuff, and I acted accordingly. I stumbled over what I wanted to say about myself and my business and stumbled all the way through the conversation. *It felt awful.*

We had, what felt like to me, a stilted, awkward conversation over salads. (I almost always order the salad—the politically correct thing to eat. Next time, I'm ordering the pizza, and I'm going to eat it. *All of it.*) I left the restaurant feeling frustrated and down about the interaction.

Looking back, I see that I stumbled over what I said about myself and my business because, to be honest, I tried to say what I thought she wanted to hear. Something that might lead me to a sale, a referral, anything. My answers were awkward because they weren't genuine. I realize now that, in truth, she was friendly and smart. She asked good questions, and I attempted to do the same.

I wonder how differently the conversation might have gone if I had chosen to be confident despite my initial impression and snap judgment of her quick scan. I wonder how differently the conversation would've gone if I'd responded to the situation with who I am and what I do *with confidence*. Maybe there would've been a lead or a referral. Maybe the conversation would've been more engaging and energetic. Maybe I would've ordered the pizza and laughed, avoiding the awkwardness of trying to cut soggy lettuce. Here's what I know though—if I had chosen to be confident despite an initial feeling, this awkward networking meeting would've been a whole lot more successful.

The point of this story is that you can see the exact moment where I decided to give up my confidence because of another person's reaction. The minute I saw her look me up and down and then assumed she didn't perceive me as being business-y (is that even a word?) enough was the minute I chose not to be confident. I let her reaction to me dictate how I felt about myself and then acted accordingly. I wasn't confident as I sat, listened, and spoke with her.

If I could go back, I would change my reaction to that moment. I would stop and remind myself that I can make the choice to be confident despite what's going on around or in front of me. I can choose to be confident despite what other people's reactions are to me. I can choose to replace the negative story running through my head with a positive one.

My friend, have you experienced a moment like this? Maybe when you were at work, when you had a job interview, or when you started a new role? Or maybe it happened somewhere else—

like walking in for the first time to volunteer at church, the PTO, your new neighborhood's garage sale? It could've been the time when you went to your significant other's family reunion and you didn't know anyone.

If it's happened to you, I want you to know that there's hope for a better outcome the next time. Because, unless you're going to be a hermit or a monk or something, you're probably going to find yourself in a situation where it will happen again. Before it does, I want to remind you that *being confident is a choice*. One you get to make, one you get to control. When you find yourself in the position where another person is looking at you and you're sensing that something's funny and you start telling yourself a story about how they're reacting to you, STOP. Stop yourself in that moment and ask yourself the question, "Is what I'm thinking true, or am I making up a story because I don't feel confident?" Then remind yourself that confidence is a choice. Think about how you look, speak, and act when you're confident, and then do it. Walk and talk like the most confident version of yourself. Listen with confidence because you know who you are and what you believe, and you don't have to worry about what someone else might be thinking about you.

You can make the choice to be confident, and you might be surprised by how easy it is once you start practicing.

P.S.

A fun follow-up to this story: I went on a
networking blind date a few weeks after this incident.
I decided to steer myself toward confidence, telling myself
I'd order whatever I darn well wanted, and I'd eat all of it.
So I ordered flaming sushi, and I ate every last bite.
Confidence for the win!

P.S.-ing my way out of the box

*"The hope of a secure and livable world lies
within disciplined nonconformists ... .
In any cause that concerns the progress of mankind,
put your faith in the nonconformist."*

—CORETTA SCOTT KING, CIVIL RIGHTS LEADER[4]

Has there ever been a moment, a window of opportunity in your life, when you had the chance to take a risk and show the world who you are? Have you had an idea that was daring—something that would push you out of your comfort zone, something that would make you stand out from the crowd when you really wanted, when you really *needed* to stand out? Have you ever thought, "Forget the way I'm *supposed* to do this, I'm going to do it *my* way!" Have you found yourself thinking, "If people only knew *this* about me, they'd be blown away!"

Did you let that moment pass?

Do you look back at that situation, that idea, that time, and think, "I wish I'd done it"? Do you think about how different things would've been if you had? If you're like me, you have lots and lots of these moments in your life. I'm going to take you way back to the early nineties, and share with you a time when I wish I would've had the confidence to do and say what I really wanted to.

I was in college and I lived with my sister, Charlotte. She's four years older, wiser, and more serious than I am. I wanted to be just like her. I moved in with her at the end of my senior year in high school. She had just gotten married, and she and her husband were renting a little house just outside of campus. Charlotte was a trooper. Can you imagine being a newlywed and letting your kid sister move in with you so she could go to college and not have to pay for student housing? You see, I was on a 21st Century Scholarship. These are scholarships that are offered in our state to kids that are on the free-lunch program. It's pretty cool. They take at-risk kids and offer them an opportunity to go to any state school if the students can manage to get through high school without doing drugs or getting into trouble, and if they keep a decent, but not unattainable, GPA. I did that. Around that time, Charlotte had decided to go back to school to finish her degree. My mom was moving out of state, and so it made financial and, honestly, emotional sense for me to move in with my sister and her husband.

Charlotte was bound and determined to keep me in school and make sure I didn't muck anything up. She helped me pick my major when I decided that nursing school was not. for. me. She checked my grades and made sure I wasn't slacking off. She made sure I got to classes, that I made it to work, and that I even had a little bit of fun while doing it. She helped me stick it out when times got tough, and it is because of her support that I went on to finish my bachelor's and master's degrees. She's amazing, my sister, and she's still my best friend and biggest cheerleader to this day.

Charlotte helped me when I went to apply for my first "real" job and had to submit a resume and a cover letter. I knew nothing about cover letters, and my employment history up to that point included two years of waitressing, a brief stint at a day care, and a few years in retail. So, she sat me down at the PC that my dad had built for us to use while we were in school. (I mean, the guy *built* it. Depending on your age, you may or may not remember the time when there was a lovely Internet dial-up sound—this was the time when you had to actually wait for the internet to work. I'm not talking about that two-second blurb where you impatiently scream, "Why is this taking so long?" I'm talking about *real* time. In this case, it took about forty-five minutes, sixty-three prayers, and two frozen burritos for our homemade computer to warm up enough for me to be able to start writing.)

I sat with Charlotte while she fed me all the "right" words to type. She sat with me patiently as I slogged out the basic three-part format of a cover letter. She remained silent when I complained about being exhausted from having to "try so hard." *She* was exhausted because she had to deal with me and my endless stream of rage-against-the-machine comments. Things like:

"This is ridiculous!"

"Why do I have to explain in three-paragraph form what position I want? Don't they look at what job I applied for?"

"You're telling me I've got to write why I'm uniquely qualified to do this job, with zero experience, and then thank this person I don't know graciously—but not too graciously—for their time?!"

"What does that even mean?"

As far as I'm concerned, Charlotte qualified for sainthood that day. How she didn't smack me down and remind me that what I was doing wasn't all that hard, I don't know. But she didn't. As I was struggle-bussing my way through the last few lines of the letter, she walked away for a minute. I got to the end and typed, "Sincerely, Alexandra." And then, on what seemed like a whim, I wrote this: "P.S. To summarize, I'm a good person, and I need a job. Love, Alex"

It made Charlotte laugh. I've always loved making her laugh. I consider it a personal accomplishment when I get her to laugh at something I say or do. There's probably some Freudian thing about older sisters and younger sisters there, but I digress.

I wrote the P.S. to be funny. Because I *am* funny. But it's taken me a long time to let that show, especially at work, where my perception has been that *I must be serious at all times to be taken seriously.* Hogwash. I missed an opportunity to be confident in who I was. And I've missed opportunities like this time and time and again. I think back to college—Alex, sitting there in an old sweatshirt in front of a bootleg computer, trying her darndest to sound like anything other than who she was because she thought she had to—because it was what the "world" was telling her to do in order to get a job.

Of course, you could argue that in order to get the job I wanted, typing a quirky P.S. would've ruined my chances. But what if, by not typing that P.S., I missed out on an opportunity to work with people who would understand me, appreciate me, and challenge me?

If I had been confident enough to leave that P.S. in my letter, who knows the people I might've gotten to meet, the opportunities I might've had. What would have happened if I'd chosen not to conform but to be confident in my ability to stand out from the crowd?

My fellow traveler, the point of this is that I don't want you to miss opportunities to be confident in yourself. You and I only get one shot in life, and I want you to take yours and use it to the fullest. I want you to be confident in who. you. are. not who you think you need to be.

My friend, there will be another moment, hopefully many other moments, where you'll have the chance to choose. You'll have the choice whether or not to say what you want to say. You'll have the choice to do the thing you want to do. You will get to choose whether or not you show up as the person who you really are. When the next moment comes, I want you to take it. I want you to choose confidence and show the world who you are.

P.S.

It's no coincidence that I wrote a P.S. all those years ago, and that I now have a company that's called PS (Practically Speaking). The Universe was trying to tell me something. The next time you feel that stir to do something outside the box, go for it. Be confident in what you're thinking!

Define "effusive"

"Love produces confidence, and adversity produces purpose."

–Eunice Kennedy Shriver, Social Worker, Children's Health
and Disability Rights Advocate, Special Olympics Founder[5]

Has this happened to you? Where a boss or someone important to you decides they don't like an aspect of your personality, so they "address" it with you (but not really)? And then, *BAM*, you're using their words to describe yourself negatively, adopting their words in their worst form (*bossy* comes to mind for women, *sensitive* for men). And then before you know it, you're trying to do all you can to stuff away that part of your personality?

Maybe you've heard comments that you're rigid, when really you're a person who has boundaries and sticks to them. Or what about labels for ourselves? How we take the words that others use to define us based on their perceptions of what they believe confidence should or shouldn't look, sound, or act like. We take up those words and then act accordingly. I mean, think about it—what sorts of things have you been told you are? Words like *introvert, extrovert, stoic, emotional*—an image pops up in your mind about someone who is introverted. You make assumptions and judgments about how such a person interacts and what he or she values. The problem with this is that it may or may not be true. The context of how you use the label, the tone with which a label gets delivered— these things matter. The person on the receiving end of the label is then left with their perception of what you think of them, which could be positive or negative.

I was about forty days into what was supposed to be my dream job when it happened to me. I got the chance to meet my boss's favorite client. My boss couldn't say enough positive things about this woman. By her descriptions, you would've thought this woman walked on water and had rainbows shooting out her ears.

I was beyond excited.

No rainbows appeared when she walked in the door, but she was beautiful, intelligent, and accomplished.

My boss told me to stay in "observation mode," which meant I was supposed to watch the session and say as little as possible.

As she left, I thanked the client for allowing me to sit in and told her I was "thrilled to meet her."

Pause here for a minute. If you haven't met me or seen me talk, you need to know that I'm expressive. My friends would say that's the understatement of the year, and they're right. When I say I'm thrilled, I look and sound thrilled.

Back to the story.

The door closed, and my boss looked at me and said, "Let's talk."

She asked me what I thought about the client, and I bubbled over with what I loved about her; she was brilliant, funny, and had an accent. I'm a sucker for an accent.

She said, "Let's talk about you."

Her words came out in a stammer as she imitated my gestures. "Alex, you're just ... so ... effusive." Her face was scrunched up—she looked disgusted. I'll never forget that look.

My chest tightened.

I didn't know what "effusive" meant, but I didn't need to. I could tell it wasn't good. I knew what she meant.

Tone it down. Hold back the energy. Don't talk "like that." Be less "Alex."

I could feel a lump rising in my throat, and I didn't want to cry in front of my new boss.

Professionals don't cry. Professionals who teach executive presence absolutely do not cry. I tried, but I couldn't stop the tears. I got up, grabbed a tissue, and tried to breathe. I came back to the table, wiping my tears away. I could see she hadn't expected my response; she just sat and stared at me. After several uncomfortable seconds of silence, she finally spoke up.

"You're your own worst critic, aren't you?"

I nodded.

She said, "Well then, we won't need to have many more conversations like this, will we?"

I nodded again.

And with that nod ... at that exact moment ... I shrunk. I packed up the parts of me that fit her description. I spent the next couple of years working hard to be anything but effusive. I wrote stuffy emails; I talked in stuffy ways; I tried to walk, talk, and act like a buttoned-up, uber-polished, non-emotional being. I was miserable. It drove me to too much Cabernet, too many Cheetos, and right on to therapy. It took me a long time to undo the damage of trying to be someone, something, other than myself. Eventually, I left that job, and I landed in a space where I didn't know what was coming next. I had choices to make about my life, my business, and my family. I needed my confidence back.

Effusive still lingered in my mind—I'd catch myself clapping loudly when a friend finished a hard workout at the gym, spontaneously hugging people after a meeting, or writing gushy emails, and I'd shame myself afterward. I'd say to myself, "Don't be so effusive, Alex." It felt awful.

Then there was a day—I can't remember exactly when, but I'm sure it was a day that I had been shaming myself for being effusive for some reason or another—when I decided to look up the exact definition of this powerful word. I don't know about you, but I've caught myself on more than one occasion using a word without a full understanding of its meaning, which can have painfully awkward results. Anyway, I decided to look it up and see what the good ol' dictionary had to say about it. I typed into the search box, and here's what I found:

"Effusive: expressing feelings of gratitude, pleasure, or approval in an unstrained or heartfelt manner. (Synonyms include: overflowing, exuberant, enthusiastic, extravagant, gushing, talkative.)"[6]

Holy cow. Talk about a stop-you-in-your-tracks, hit-me-over-the-head-with-a-skillet, crazy-wonderful moment. I read those words and thought, *That's me.* And I began to cry. I cried and I laughed, and I kind of wanted to smack myself around for a bit because, oh my gosh, *why hadn't I looked it up sooner?* I could've saved myself some heartache. When I read those words, I knew that I am, in fact, *effusive.* I knew in that moment that I must own being effusive and that I must be confident in my effusiveness. It's part of who I am. It's part of what others love about me. It's part of how I want people to remember me when I'm gone.

I decided to be confident in being effusive. I decided I was no longer going to allow someone else's negative spin on a word make me less than who I am. I've made effusive mine in the most gushing, enthusiastic, and overflowing way possible.

In my initial experience with the word, my boss's interpretation of the word was negative. No doubt. However, there are so many positives in that definition that ring true to me. If we're going to be confident, we must choose to focus on the aspects of ourselves that make us feel confident. When I feel confident, I act effusively, gushingly, gratefully—basically all of the emotions come out of my face. But I'm more than that too. I'm clear, I'm concise, and I can command the heck out of a room. The lesson here is that it doesn't matter how someone else labels you, it's how you label yourself that matters most, and if you get to choose the label, why would you choose anything other than confident?

Look, there are still moments in certain situations where I find it difficult to be my confident self. I'd be lying to you if I told you otherwise. I still have times when I pull into the parking lot of a business where I'm doing work, or I get to a new friend's house and

I feel a twinge in my gut about driving up in my minivan. A voice whispers in my head, "Are they going to think less of me because I don't drive a fancy car?" It's in those moments that I have the choice to believe the thoughts that roll through my head or I can choose to be confident in who I am, and let me tell you, when I choose anything other than my truest self, it shows. And vice versa. You may not have a single word—like effusive—that describes you, and that's OK. Whatever makes you *you* is special. Whatever inspires confidence within you is what will get you further down the road of the confident life you're aiming to live.

P.S.
Steer toward confidence with the words
you use to describe yourself.

I blame elementary school and Brené Brown for this

"My motto about the unknown is: You never know if you want it until you try it. So, when you see an opportunity, seize it. When you spot a problem, fix it. When you want something, ask for it."

–KATE MCCUE, MASTER MARINER, FIRST AMERICAN FEMALE
CRUISE SHIP CAPTAIN, LIFE-LONG SEA ADVENTURER[7]

You've been programmed to ask for permission. Seriously, it started with school, and now Brené's got you writing permission slips to yourself. *Sigh.* If you're reading this and wondering who Brené Brown is, let me take this moment to fill you in: Brené is a leadership guru. I mean like, Oprah-sized guru in the world of leadership development. She's a world-renowned speaker on vulnerability. She was made famous by her TED Talk on vulnerability. My reference to her here is based on a story I heard her tell about meeting Oprah for the first time and how she wrote a permission slip for herself to enjoy the experience. She encourages people to do the same—to write permission slips for yourself to feel, do, or say something.

While I appreciate the story and her encouragement of others to do what works for her, I don't agree with the extra step it requires. Too many women and men, especially those who have experienced any form of abuse, have been placed in positions in their life where they've been forced to ask permission for the most basic human needs. Telling adults to give themselves permission still places an adult in the position of "asking." My point here is that you are an adult—you don't need to ask. Putting yourself in the position to ask for permission or grant permission to do the thing or be the thing you want wastes energy and can even delay or stop you on your road to confidence.

Please keep in mind that I'm encouraging you to feel confident enough in who you are and what you want to do (or not do) that you're able to make decisions without the need to give yourself permission to make the choice you know you want to make.

Here's what I'm betting is going on with you right now: You've got some "thing" you're not doing because you're waiting for permission. You want to "do something," "be something," or "say something." It could be something in your personal life, at work, at home, with friends, with family, or at church. And if you're like many of people I come into contact with every day, you're waiting for somebody's permission to do the thing you want to do.

Maybe you want to write a blog, start a new project, or create a new widget. It could be that you want to try out a new hobby, exercise routine, or join a new group. But you don't because you're waiting for someone to give you permission. And it's killing your confidence. It's killing your confidence because you already know you want to do it, but you're holding back because we're programmed from the time we're born to ask someone else if we *can* do something. And for a while, it's really important that we do that. We can't have elementary schoolers running amok. (The amount of glue consumption and toy destruction would be insane.) We can't have teenagers taking off with the car whenever they please. (Although they do that sometimes anyway.) And there's the very real truth at work and at home that says we can't make all decisions unilaterally, unless we're aiming to get fired, divorced, or create a dictatorship. (Please don't do that; dictators aren't cool.)

But when it comes to making decisions about what you want to do, how you want to be, and what you want to say, you know what you want. *So do it already.* Continuing to seek out and ask others for permission as a way of affirming what you already know wastes your time and someone else's. It's like stopping to ask for directions over and over again on a trip where you've already got the GPS running and you're on the right road. It doesn't make sense.

When you know what you want to do, be confident in your decision. You don't need permission slips anymore. Go do, say, or be the thing—confidently, of course.

P.S.

Confidence is a choice. You can choose to be confident right now; no permission slip required.

Rearview Reflection

Remember: When in doubt, steer toward confidence.

OK, it's time for you to answer a few questions. I encourage you to make your notes right here in this book so you can refer back to your answers later. Don't sweat—there are no right or wrong answers. These questions are here to help motivate you to choose confidence.

ANSWER THE FOLLOWING QUESTIONS

1. What has stopped you from being/feeling confident today?
2. What do you need to do to make it easy to choose confidence?
3. How will you feel if you choose to be confident right now?
4. How much more productive will you be if you choose to be confident in yourself?
5. How will your life improve if you choose to be confident today?

CHAPTER TWO

ROAD RULE 2: KEEP YOUR EYES ON THE ROAD IN FRONT OF YOU.

"Forget the competition and focus on your goal."

–Milka Duno, Model, Naval Engineer, Stock Car Driver[8]

Introduction

*I*t's so easy, isn't it? To look at other people and compare yourself to them? To look at your phone and see what others are doing, give yourself FOMO (fear of missing out)? To look at what others have and say, "I wish I had that. I wish I could do what they do. I wish I were like her"? It's likely that you're doing this with the people you're closest to: your family, friends, and coworkers. Your neighbors, your friends on social media, the folks at your gym, church, or social club. Is this you? It's generally not the celebrities or influencers so much—their lives seem so far removed—but even they sometimes creep in and cause you to wonder what it would be like to do ... to have ... to be.

Comparison is a human condition, one that's been around for as long as we have.

Social comparison theory has been around since the 1950s and suggests that we make comparisons as a way of evaluating ourselves. Our brains are wired to look at someone else and make an instant judgment that goes back to our caveman days of needing to make those judgments so we could protect ourselves. Except now we don't live in the caveman days (I'm sure glad I drive a minivan versus being chased by lions), and the act of social comparison isn't so helpful anymore. In fact, there's research that supports the idea that chronic social comparison leads to depression, substance abuse, and anxiety. If you've ever found yourself in front of the TV with a jar of peanut butter after scrolling through social media, then you know what I'm talking about.

The problem I've found with comparing myself to other people is that every time I do, I'm killing my confidence. When I get tied up—comparing myself to other people and looking at who's got more money, more friends, more awards, more skills, more personality—I'm focusing on the exact opposite of what *I* want, which is to feel confident about who *I* am. I've wasted a lot of time chasing after what confidence looks like on someone else instead of figuring out what confidence looks and feels like on me. From trying to build a body that's not mine, build a career that's not mine, and trying to look, speak, and act like someone other than who I am, I've tried to acquire all the things that might suggest I'm confident but are actually false. Because at the end of the day, *things* don't bring confidence. Confidence comes from within.

Keeping our eyes on the road in front of us is a challenge. In an ever-distractible, see-everything-about-everybody kind of world, it's a daunting challenge. And it's one that we must continually practice, fail, learn, and relearn in our effort to be confident.

This lesson is so critical that I want to remind you in every way possible to keep your eyes on the road in front of you. I want you to understand this, because what I know for sure is that your confidence will not look, sound, feel, or be like anyone else's. Here's why: there isn't a single person in this world who has had the exact same struggles, challenges, victories, or hairstyles as you. There isn't a single person in this world who has the unique combination of intellect, talent, and spirit you have. You're not just one in a million. You're a never-gonna-happen-again, only-occurs-once-in-the-universe, will-never-be-featured-again-on-Earth person. It cannot be that your confidence will look like someone else's because there's only one *you*. So, to keep you from losing the confidence you've chosen, and to keep you moving forward, you must keep your eyes on the road in front of you—not in someone else's lane, right-of-way, or road trip. You are in the driver's seat—you choose the vehicle, you choose the path, and you make sure it's what makes *you* feel confident.

P.S.
Staying in your own lane will ensure you
get to where you're supposed to go when
you're supposed to get there.

Social media scrolling

"Say no with a smile."

–Venus Williams, First African American Woman to be Number
One in world tennis, Pro Tennis Player, Serial Entrepreneur[9]

I feel like social media could be an entire book—it probably is an entire book, but I haven't looked on Amazon. That's a rabbit hole I can't afford to go down. This is a crash course on confidence, after all. If you use social media, I'm sure you can relate to how it can, if we let it, play a significant role—a negative role—in how confident we feel about our ourselves, our choices, and our lives.

I was scrolling through LinkedIn, like I do, checking out what's trending in my neck of the woods—you know, making myself a well-rounded professional. In other words, avoiding doing stuff I should be doing while I hide from my kid in the bathroom. (Yes, sometimes I hide from my kid. I don't mind telling you that. Momma needs a break from time to time, and sometimes the bathroom is where I get it. Judge me all you want.) Anyway, I'm scrolling along, and BAM, there's *the post*. You know the post I'm talking about. The one by a friend, someone you work with, or somebody you just sort of know. It has the "perfect" picture—a funny one-liner or a description of something cool that you weren't a part of.

It's a great post. With fantastic people. Doing awesome things. Your first thought goes something like, "Aw man, I didn't know about this." Then maybe you go to, "DANG IT, I want to be there!" Next, "Why *wasn't* I there?" Then, "Man, I should be doing that." And finally, "I wish I were like—" And then BOOM, all of a sudden, you've deemed yourself inadequate, and any confidence you started the day with is now in the toilet. Have you been here before? It's called by many names: FOMO, envy, social comparison, and even jealousy. And it stinks. It sucks out all the good feels you had about yourself.

If you're like me, when this happens, I get a sudden urge to try to add more to what I'm already doing because now that I've seen someone else doing, having, or being something on social media, I now want to do, have, be what others are doing, having, and being. This tends to be especially true for me if it's something I'm not good at, not doing, or have never tried. It's like, because they're doing it, I have to do it too, or I'm somehow less than they are. So I start planning and scheming to do all sorts of stuff:

"Bob is doing underwater bungie jumping. I should too!"

"Geez, I never thought of making dog footprints to memorialize each year of Max's life—I'll add that to my list of to-dos."

"Everyone I know is making videos in their car. I'm going to make videos of me talking about random stuff in my VAN!"

I could go on and on, but it's ridiculous and I'll tell you why. I can't run businesses and simultaneously create picture-perfect Pinterest meals, attend networking events, write blogs, vlog, drive the kids to sports, volunteer at church, and sit on three boards, and, and, and ... you get my point. I can't be everything to everybody or be a part of everything. I've got to focus on what's most important for my family, my work, and my friends. Despite what I see on social media. No one, my friend, is everything to everybody. If someone you know is claiming to be that, be wary. Be very wary. That's called *overconfidence*, and you don't want to be that person. Nope. Not a chance.

So how do we deal with social comparison and sudden urges to do more to boost our confidence when it's been shaken by seeing someone else being something that we aren't? Good question. For many of us, our entire world is online, which makes social-media abstinence a no-go. Maybe you rely on your online presence to share pictures with your family, or you've got teens who need to be monitored (like. a. hawk.), or it's beneficial for your business. Or maybe you just like it because ... puppy videos.

While banning social media from your life entirely might seem like the right way to go in theory, it's not likely a viable option. First, we've got to recognize that those feelings are normal and everyone gets them. Everyone—even Oprah. Your parents and your best friend—they feel the same pressure. It's part of being human.

Something you *can* reasonably do to stop yourself before you rush into a new undertaking is to ask yourself if you're already doing everything you need to be doing *well*. If you're like me, the answer is almost always *no*. No. I am not. I already have a graveyard of half-finished, half-hearted projects that have left me feeling strung out, stressed out, and, quite frankly, like I'm not *enough*—the furthest possible place from feeling confident. If that's the case, why on Earth would you take on something new?

The next thing you can ask yourself is: What are the things I have been doing well that I LOVE, the things that light MY fire, that make me feel happy and fulfilled? What are the things I'm already doing that make me feel good about myself? That make me feel confident about who I am?

Once you've answered those questions, I want you to remind yourself to keep working on the stuff you need and actually *want* to do before you take on one. more. thing. (Poor Max will have to accept that phases of his life won't be documented in plaster molds hung on the wall.)

These two simple questions will help you get back on the road and focused on what's important to you—not the illusion of what's important to you based on someone else's life, goals, and current situation on social media. Because, to be honest, everyone else's lives are none of your business—or mine. Of course, you can take on challenges and try new things, but you need to do it when it makes sense for YOU. When you can feel confident that it's the right choice for you.

So, the next time you find yourself hiding in the bathroom, binging on social media with a sudden urge to try something that looks good in someone else's life, STOP. Put the phone down and remind yourself that you need to be confident in what *you're* doing. If you're going to maintain confidence in yourself, you've got to keep your eyes on the road in front of you.

> **P.S.**
> If you are a social-media guru, Pinterest queen, or Insta celeb,
> I'm not telling you to change any of that. I am telling
> you that if you feel yourself losing confidence because
> you see what other people are doing, stop looking.
> You're on the right track for *you*. Be confident in what you do.

**"Comparison is the thief of joy until you realize
you're better than everyone else."**

—Carmen Rufatto-Teenager, lover of all social media, and ravioli junkie

My kid said that.

Carmen was in eighth grade at the time. You know, that glorious time in our lives when acne and comparison problems are rampant.

I was enjoying a rare moment when I had her undivided attention, a.k.a. we were in the van and she couldn't get away. We were just talking—nothing specific, and I can't even remember why I said, *"comparison is the thief of joy,"* but her response made me laugh.

She went on to say, "OK, OK, I don't mean it that way. But, Mom, it feels good to know you're doing better than someone else."

She's right; it does.

Comparison doesn't steal joy. Feeling bad about who I am, how I performed, or the state of my circumstances—that steals my joy. There's a difference. I can't blame comparison for something I'm choosing to do. I am the only one in charge of my feelings.

P.S.

Please note: I'm not encouraging you to think or say that you're better than everyone else. I am saying that it's OK to look around from time to time and acknowledge that you're doing well. That maybe, just maybe, you've gotten some things right, and it's OK that it feels good. Sometimes we spend so much time comparing ourselves to other people who we think are "better" than us, we forget to take stock of our own successes and accomplishments and to let them fuel our confidence.

"What is it about you that I don't like about me?"

Oh, good old Dr. Phil. If you don't recognize the name, let me Phil you in (pun intended). Dr. Phil is a popular daytime talk show host who specializes in family and personal drama. He uses his superpowers of psychology to assess people on the spot and mediate conversations—very personal conversations—for all to view. In other words, he's a reality show host who gets people to talk about their most personal problems on TV. I spent a good deal of my free time in college watching Oprah, Dr. Phil, and Dr. Oz. They were my trifecta of personal enlightenment at the time. Feel free to judge me if you like—I don't mind. But one of my favorite Dr. Phil-isms has stuck with me through the years: *"What is it about you that I don't like about me?"* If you're not familiar with Dr. Phil, he uses this phrase a lot when he's interviewing guests on his show and they're complaining about someone else.

It sort of stings a little when you think about it, doesn't it? It's the first question I ask myself when I get that funny little twinge in my gut that says, "I don't think I like him/her." When I get that feeling, the next thing that usually happens is I start to overanalyze or criticize someone's behavior. I find it happens to me the most with women, and while I'm not a psychologist, I'm guessing it's easier to project my stuff onto someone who happens to be the same gender.

It's happened to me before, when I was out with friends and one of them, in my not so humble opinion, was taking up too much of the conversation with her "issues." She wasn't giving anyone else a chance to talk, and she made it all about her. I tried to demonstrate my patience, but as the conversation continued, I started to think, "Sheesh, I wish she'd stop talking and let someone else have a turn." And then the next thought floated through my mind: "Does she even realize how many times she's said 'I' in the last fifteen minutes?" And by the end I was thinking, "All she talks about is herself—how gross." Sound familiar? Or is it just me?

The truth is, if I had a dollar for every time I've had this thought, I'd be as rich as Dr. Phil. And, man oh man, would I have the minivan souped-up and looking extra fine. Unpleasant as it is, I find myself repeating this pattern of thought often. I don't like admitting it, but it's true. It's my super-judgmental, ultra-superior, jerk of a self coming out in full force (or at least speaking up in full force in my head). And what I've learned is that, when I'm thinking stuff like this, it's generally because I'm feeling insecure. It's not pretty, but it's true. It's easier to find flaws in other people than it is to find them in myself. If I'm bothered by the friend who is taking up too much time with her issues, it's because I know, on some level, at some time, I've been the friend who has done exactly that, and I feel insecure about it.

Insecurity and confidence can't live in the same space. When we're feeling confident about ourselves, we really don't care about what anyone else is doing. We aren't comparing ourselves to other people and judging them. When we choose to feel confident in ourselves, we're free to let others be themselves.

The next time you find yourself with a twinge in your gut, when thoughts about how another person is acting start to overtake you and you feel judgment coming on, or the next time you find yourself *really* bothered by someone else's behavior, stop and ask yourself: "What is it about me that I don't like about you?" What are *you* doing that's bugging you?

P.S.

Comparison can get ugly when it turns into judgment of the people around you. Don't look for ways to make yourself feel better by finding the flaws in other people's behavior or words. When you're truly happy and confident with who you are, you'll find it's easier to fight the urge to compare.

What we miss when we compare

"All tides rise when we support one another in pursuit of our dreams."

–Natalie Franke, Community Builder, Brain Tumor Warrior, Wedding Photographer-turned-Creative[10]

It was my second time attending DisruptHR Indianapolis, a TED Talk-inspired event focused on disrupting the world of human resources. These events are so cool. They're held in various trendy locations throughout our city, and they offer food, beverages, and good networking. Ten speakers take the stage, where, in five minutes, they're challenged with sharing a disruptive idea using twenty auto-advancing slides. (Auto-advancing means they have no control, and the slides move forward every fifteen seconds whether they like it or not.) I've done one myself, and it was hard. Super hard. Nail-biting, screaming-in-my-office kind of hard. I'm glad I did it—I'd almost call it fun, but I gotta tell ya, it was way more fun to be there supporting one of my clients and cheering on all the other speakers. Indianapolis is a big small town, and so many of the speakers who were there are people I consider friends as well as colleagues.

If I haven't said it before, I LOVE watching people speak. I'm the gal who sits in the front row at conferences and workshops. I binge-watch TED Talks, and on many days, I've got motivational speakers playing in the minivan while I'm driving. So basically, this event was like Christmas for me. I got to stand in the back, watching people I care about doing something they love—speaking about things that matter to them. Call me a geek; I don't care.

Like most human interactions, this could've turned into a competition. What is it about us that makes us turn everything into a competition? I mean, seriously, I don't know about you, but I could make returning a grocery cart a competition. *I see you, Lexus driver, you have no idea who you're messing with here.*

Anyway, most of the speakers at this event are like me—small business owners. Most of us are in various stages of our careers but close enough that it's easy to compare. Too easy, in fact. It would've been all too easy on an evening like this for things to turn into an alcohol-fueled comparison gossip fest.

You might have been to something like this before—a party, neighborhood gathering, networking event. There are whispers in the background. People are saying things like:

"Aw man, did you see what she did? That was something."

"He was off his game tonight, huh? He's going to be embarrassed about that tomorrow."

"I mean, if it were me, I would've done it this way ...."

How gross.

Gross but true, because it's oh, so easy to sit back and judge. Oh, so easy to sit back and compare ourselves to someone else.

And what good does that do for you, for the other person, and for the people around you who are watching you and wondering if you're going to talk about them behind their backs as well? You don't want to do that. You aren't meant to do that. You're meant to do so much more than compare. You're meant to be confident in yourself, and when you are, you're able to support other people without all the comparison.

As I stood in the back of the room that night with my friends, it would have been so easy to compare ourselves to the speakers. It would have been so easy to make thinly veiled comments that sound like commentary but are really a way to voice our insecurities when we see someone doing something and wonder if they're "better" than we are.

I'm proud to say we didn't do that. Instead of comparing, we rotated in and out of seats, standing where the other speakers could see us. Instead of comparing, we cheered for each speaker. Instead of comparing, we hugged them as they walked off the stage. Instead of comparing, we said, "Man, did you see THAT? How cool was THAT?"

If you've ever been a part of something like this—a part of celebrating others—you know that this kind of spirit is contagious. It contributes to the success of the event. People respond to the energy you create by being supportive, not competitive with each other. It brings everyone's confidence up, and *that* is magic, my friend. Simply magic.

And that kind of magic rubs off. Confident people build each other up, not tear each other down. Confident people look at what others have with admiration, not jealousy. Confident people know that by comparing too much, they miss the opportunity to acknowledge their own success or to support someone else in theirs. When in doubt, keep your eyes on the road in front of you and cheer for the other drivers, whether they're behind you, ahead of you, or right beside you along the way.

P.S.
Another person's talents, skills, or interests don't negate yours.
Be confident in who you are and what you do.

You are one in a million or trillion or some crazy number like that

"My whole self is here. My values, my passion, my sense of urgency."
–Rose Marcario, Activist and CEO, Financial Wiz, Mindful Leader[11]

My friend, Mike, is one of the nicest guys on the planet. Like me, he's a speaker, trainer, and author. And he's great at everything he does. He's funny, self-effacing, and sharp. He asks great questions and listens intently. He's one of those guys who makes you feel like you've learned something every time you walk away from a conversation.

We were chatting about an upcoming event where we were both slated to speak. We were talking about the trials and tribulations of speaking—tough audiences, feedback forms, losing your place—when he asked me: *"Who do you compare yourself to as a speaker?"*

It's a question I get a lot, and it's tough for me to answer for a few reasons. One, there are a zillion great speakers in the world; two, sometimes when people ask you this question, what they really want to do is debate with you about who *they* think is a great speaker (I'm not down for that—people like who they like, and that's cool with me); and three—this one is probably the most important—my favorite speakers are the folks who show up as themselves, the ones where you can tell it's not a show, that what they're sharing comes from the heart and that they believe and feel every last thing they're saying. The truth about those folks is that they're often the people who *aren't* celebrities, politicians, or famous CEOs—they're people in our lives who happen to speak publicly and are generally not professional speakers.

You'll remember from earlier in this book that I've gotten myself into trouble trying to be something—or someone—I'm not, so I was careful as I answered his question.

I told him, "I work hard *not to compare myself to others.*"

"Yeah, I get that, but like, who do you watch and try *to be like?*" he asked again. Mike has a quiet persistence about him, which is both charming and frustrating.

I told him that I've spent too many years comparing myself to other speakers—and, quite frankly, other people—trying to imitate their actions, their words, their styles. I've spent my fair share of time "trying on" things I've seen others do. I've copied gestures and phrases and even imitated the way others say their words *(Ooh, she drew out her "s" like* thisss—*maybe I should do that too?).* I'm embarrassed to admit that I even tried to tell someone else's story during a talk like it was mine. I had the person's permission and encouragement, but it still felt gross, because at the end of the day, the person who *I am* shows up, regardless of my efforts to try to act like someone else. And I did all of that because I didn't feel confident in my own style, my own stories, or my own abilities.

I'm not sure Mike got the answer he wanted, but it was the truth. Comparison, if you let it, will get in the way or—even worse—stop you from being the confident person who you're meant to be.

Trust me, I know that we naturally look to those around us—our parents, our teachers our friends, and our colleagues to learn about how to interact and present ourselves to others. And it's OK as long as it doesn't cause us to shift into self-doubt, negative self-thoughts, or even stop us from trying at all. I mean, think about it. Have you ever thought: *"She's so much better than me at* [insert anything here] *... I could never ...."*

Have you ever said those words out loud? Or: *"I'll never be as good as him, so why even try?"*

These are all words of death for confidence. Comparison becomes a problem when it stops you from being confident in who you are, and isn't that the opposite of what you want? Don't you want to be confident in who you are and how you do what you do?

Listen, on the road of life, *there will always be someone who's ahead of you and someone who's behind.* That's *reality*, and I have yet to win an argument with reality. It doesn't matter what everyone else is doing or how someone else does what they do if you're confident in who you are. When you catch yourself in the trap of looking at someone else and trying to be like them, stop. Focus on being confident in yourself. You are already one in a million, my friend. No one else can be you. No one can do what you do the way you do it. Be confident in this knowledge.

P.S.

If you're struggling with confidence, if you find yourself stuck in a spot where you're eyeball-deep in comparing yourself to a coworker, a friend, or someone in your family, get out a piece of paper and a pencil right now and write down three things that make you unique—truly unique. Now put that list where you can always see it, so that it can remind you that you are unlike anyone else on this planet and the world needs you to show up exactly as you are. *Don't become so busy trying to be one in a million that you forget you already ARE.*

Remember: Keep your eyes on the road in front of you.

ANSWER THE FOLLOWING QUESTIONS

1. Who are you comparing yourself to today, and why?
2. What do you need to do to make it easy for you to focus on yourself instead of someone else?
3. How will you feel if you choose to measure your success by your own standards rather than some else's?
4. How much more productive will you be if you choose to focus on your success versus someone else's?
5. How will your professional life and your personal life improve if you choose to focus on yourself?

CHAPTER THREE

ROAD RULE 3: WHEN SOMEONE CATCHES YOU
SINGING AT A STOP LIGHT, SMILE AND WAVE!

"It's not healthy to keep a 'game face' on all the time … It's OK to have a meltdown. As leaders, the best example we can set is how to recover."

–DANIELLE WEISBERG AND CARLY ZAKIN, MILLENIAL MEDIA INNOVATORS[12]

Introduction

You are human and, therefore, subject to awkward moments. *You* are awkward. *I* am awkward. *Everyone* is awkward. Are some people better at hiding their awkward than others? Of course. Are some folks exceptional at making uncomfortable situations even more awkward? Yup. You might be one of those folks, and if you're not sure, ask your family—they'll be more than happy to tell you. Don't you just love folks who own their awkwardness and make it OK for everyone else in the room? That's confidence right there, to take what's sometimes painfully uncomfortable and make it OK—not just sweep it under the rug or pretend it didn't happen.

Let's talk about this for a moment, shall we? If you've been alive for more than a few minutes, you've had something like the following happen to you: your stomach growls loudly during a conversation; you go to give someone a high five and they don't put their hand up; you're riding in the elevator and you miss your floor; you call someone by the wrong name; you trip over nothing in public; you just don't get the joke your friend told but you laugh anyway; you wave at someone who wasn't waving at you; the waiter comes up and asks you a question right as you put a bite in your mouth; you say goodbye to someone, only to realize that they're going the same way …. Are you cringing yet? I'm cringing.

What do you do when something awkward happens? Do you pretend it didn't? Do you make up a little white lie to cover it up? Do you own the moment, own your awkwardness in all of its glory?

I don't know about you, but I really like people who own awkward moments because then it's easier to own mine. People who are able to laugh off the noisy stomach; say with a smile, "I'm sorry, I forgot your name"; or laugh at themselves when they trip in public serve as "awkward" role models.

Think back to the last time you were with a group of acquaintances—maybe folks in your neighborhood who you sort of know but not really. You're all standing in someone's backyard, chatting about the kids or your jobs. A neighbor (we'll call her neighbor #1) walks up. You know her face, but you've completely forgotten her name. She says, "Hi, (insert your name here)," because of course she knows *your* name, and you start to panic. You say, "Oh, hiiiiii! How are *you*?" while you frantically search your mind for her name. You maintain a slightly awkward conversation, but you can't really focus on what's being said because you're shaming yourself for not being a better neighbor. You're mentally committing to learning the names of everyone who lives in the entire neighborhood before the next gathering.

To make things worse, neighbor #2 walks up, says hello, and asks to be introduced to neighbor #1. You're wishing for a sinkhole to open up in the neighborhood right now. You're BUSTED. Now you've got to own that you have no idea what neighbor #1's name is, and you've made it even more awkward by letting a conversation go on like you did. Now I'm really cringing.

This part of the book is exceptionally important because part of being confident is owning the fact that you are human and, therefore, have awkward human moments. Pretending you don't generally has the opposite effect of confidence; ignoring these uncomfortable moments tends to make things worse. If you're going to be confident, truly confident, you're going to have to own as many of your awkward moments as possible. You know, like when you get caught at a stoplight singing at the top of your lungs, putting on your mascara, or checking Facebook. It sounds simple to just give in to the awkwardness, but it's not always easy. I could write an entire book on the awkward moments I've experienced in my life. The good news for you is that I'm not planning to do that—I'm merely sharing a few here to illustrate my point. Enjoy the cringe!

P.S.
Awkwardness is relatable.
A universal condition we've all
experienced in one way or another.

There's nothing unique about me

"Style — all who have it share one thing: originality."

–Diana Vreeland, Fashion Editor, Society Girl, Global Tastemaker[13]

In 2018, I was a guest on the Amplify Indy podcast. Harrison Painter and Joshua Bach are the hosts, and their mission is to help people, organizations, and businesses become the best version of themselves. They had me on to talk about professional presence, storytelling, and public speaking. The conversation was what you'd typically expect out of a business podcast. The hosts ask you questions about who you are, what you do, how you got started, biggest lessons learned, etc. The conversation was good, and I got through it without any major faux pas (a.k.a. awkward moments).

That was, until we got to the end and Harrison asked me this: "In ninety seconds, tell us what's *unique* about you."

I find this type of question super fun to ask other people and annoyingly difficult to answer myself.

Crud.

My first thought was, *There's nothing unique about me at all.* And finding myself stuck in a moment of panic while the hosts talked, the first answer to pop out of my mouth was:

"I like Cheetos." Tasty, delicious, not unique.

Followed by: "I like Cheetos, and I find them especially wonderful *when paired with Cabernet.*"

Awkward.

Being put on the spot can be tricky. Have you ever been asked a question by a stranger, a close friend, a colleague, or maybe your boss, and you panic a little because you didn't see it coming? Have there been times when you've been asked a question and you have nothing to say, you don't feel like you can or should say something, or you need more time to think about your answer? It's hard, isn't it?

If you're like me, you worry that the answer you give won't measure up to what others want to hear. Or you worry that if you go with your first thought, you might not sound as interesting or intelligent as you'd like to. Maybe you worry that your answer will leave you looking like you're bragging or arrogant. So then, in response to those worries, you come up with an answer that is awkward (at least by your standards). The response tumbles out of your mouth and then you're left with a split-second decision. Do you own the awkward or try to let it pass?

My friend, when you're in doubt about an awkward thing you've done or said, when you're unsure of what to do next, when you're in the midst of feeling like those around you are uncomfortable with your awkwardness—any time you're in doubt, the best possible response is to own your awkwardness.

Here's why: there isn't a person on this Earth who has lived and interacted with humans for any amount of time who *hasn't* experienced what awkward feels like. While the people you're dealing with may not have had the exact same experience as you, they definitely know how you're feeling. If you can get ahold of yourself in the midst of an uncomfortable situation and own it, you're going to experience two important things: one, the relief from trying to hide your awkwardness which, in and of itself, is an awkward thing to do and can often have the adverse effect of making things even worse. And two, you'll make it OK for the people around you to own up to similar moments they've experienced (a.k.a. you'll now share an awkward bond).

While it may seem counterintuitive that owning your awkwardness breeds confidence, it really isn't. Being true to yourself and giving yourself grace in uncomfortable moments—those are confidence moves. You're smart enough to acknowledge others and the impact of your behavior, and you gain confidence by realizing you aren't the only one who's ever fumbled through life.

While we were still recording the podcast, I told Harrison about my struggle to answer his on-the-spot question, and I owned up to the awkwardness I felt about my Cheetos and Cabernet answer. I suspect I'm not the only person who loves Cheetos and has struggled to answer an unexpected question, and I'd like to think that because I owned that moment, I made it OK for someone else to say, "Ah, me too!" We had a good laugh and moved on. It was, indeed, a podcasting success for all of us.

P.S.
There will be times when you find it virtually impossible to immediately own an awkward moment, and that's OK. But know that when you do address that moment or come back around to it, you'll probably ease someone else's mind about their own experience. Let this universal condition fuel your confidence rather than hinder it.

Ever tried to Skype in Arabic?

"Sometimes your limitations can be a launching pad into an unexpected story."
–Dana Tanamachi, Author, Multi-dimensional Designer, Typographer[14]

How many times in your life have you told a little white lie to save yourself from sounding awkward? How many times have you fudged the truth just a bit so you don't feel so weird in an encounter with someone else? If you're being honest, you tell lots of them on a daily basis. Little white lies like:

- *"Of course I remember you!"* (When you run into someone in the grocery store and they clearly know who you are but you have zero idea who they are.)
- *"Of course that makes sense!"* (When someone is explaining something to you, and you don't want to look dumb but also don't understand.)
- *"Traffic was terrible!"* (When you're late to meet a friend—again—because you either a.) don't really want to do the thing you're doing but feel obligated to so you waited until the last possible minute to leave, or b.) tried to do *just one more thing* before you left—a.k.a. not prioritizing where you were supposed to be—and left at the last minute.)

If you're like me, you tell the little white lie and let the awkward moment pass. You hope you've pulled it off and faked your way through the moment, sparing yourself and the other person from the discomfort that awkwardness brings. Maybe you think about it later on and wonder, "Could they tell I was lying?" Or you go home and tell your spouse, roommate, or friend about the moment, and you laugh because they've had a very similar experience. You know and I know that we've all had these moments and that we've tried to cover our way out of them. Maybe you even feel a little guilty about not being honest, about not owning up to the awkward in the moment.

Have you looked back and wondered what would've happened if you'd just told the other person the truth? Or have you ever had one of those moments where you were brave enough to tell the other person the truth? Have you ever acknowledged the awkward truth of a situation and had it work out for the better? It can happen, you know; you just have to be brave enough to skip the white lie and own what's really happening in the moment.

Here's a good example of when I really, really didn't want to own up to the awkwardness that was going on in my life because I didn't want to admit I was struggling with technology ...

again. If you've ever had the uncomfortable, cringe-worthy, darn near mortifying experience of having technology fail you at an inopportune moment—perhaps trying to have a tough conversation over FaceTime with a loved one, giving a presentation and having your oh, so cool video fail, or shooting off an email too quickly because your fingers hit the wrong keys—you'll appreciate this.

In my mind, technology at its best is supposed to help me avoid some of the common missteps and mishaps that occur in everyday, face-to-face conversation. At least, that's what I *think* it's supposed to do. I mean, isn't that why very smart people developed tools like spell-check? Technology is supposed to help me connect quickly, almost instantly, with anyone around the world. It's supposed to make my life easier, make my work go faster and—as an added bonus—make me look really, really cool. And for the most part, technology does exactly what it promises—that is, it does, right up until it fails me. Or is it that I fail it? I'm still not sure.)

Here's what happened. It was *thirty minutes* before I was supposed to be a podcast guest on a show with a guy I'd met on social media. He's a professor of public speaking in San Antonio, and I'd admired his posts for a while. He had posted, looking for speakers who would be willing to serve as guests on his podcast to share their stories about public speaking successes and failures. I put in my request and he accepted, and I was excited. I was still very, very new in the world of public speaking, so I was thrilled to get the chance to talk to a seasoned expert about a topic I love. He sent me all of the required information and told me we'd be having our conversation over Skype. Easy enough. I had an old Skype account—all I would need to do is pull it up, find a quiet place to chat with him, and we'd be off to the races.

If only life were that simple. I pulled up my account with a full thirty minutes before we were supposed to talk, and for a reason that is still unbeknownst to me, my Skype account was in a different language. What language, you ask? Well, I had to look up the words online to figure that out. Turns out it was Arabic. I don't speak Arabic, read Arabic, and for goodness' sake, I didn't even recognize it. My four years of high school Spanish over twenty years ago wasn't helpful either. I panicked.

I frantically hit buttons to try to switch the language settings, which turns out to be especially challenging when you can't read the settings, and the last time you used your Skype was three years ago. I again turned to the great Google to see if it could offer assistance to me, scouring the Skype help page for a solution. The not-so-helpful help page instructed me to "go to tools and change the language setting." Which I would have gladly done, if I could have identified the word "tools" in the jumbled writing on the screen. Thanks for nothing, Skype help page.

The clock was ticking down fast, and I was panicked. I mean, how dumb would I look admitting that I can't figure out my Skype account? I'm supposed to be a professional, an adult, a put-together person who doesn't experience strange issues like a malfunction in a Skype account. *Be cool, Alex, be cool.*

I started to message Steven with a perfectly acceptable little white lie. "Dear Steven: My apologies, I've had an unexpected client issue come up that I must attend to. I'll need to reschedule our podcast interview at a later date."

It sounds good, right? Perfectly acceptable, not a bit awkward, and ultra-professional.

Except it was a total lie.

I didn't want to lie. Even if it was a "perfectly acceptable" little white lie. Even if it wouldn't matter in the long run. But on this particular day, in this particularly awkward set of circumstances, I couldn't do it. I couldn't tell the little while lie that would save me the awkwardness of my truth in the moment. My Skype was in Arabic, I didn't know how to fix it, and the Skype help page wasn't helpful. That was the awkward truth and I wanted—I needed—to tell him the truth. I needed to be me, and so I was.

So, I sent him this message:

Dear Steven,

I'm in the process of determining why my Skype app only reads in Arabic. Skype site not helpful as it says, "Go to tools and change language setting," which seems easy enough. However, when one doesn't speak Arabic, it's difficult to determine what symbol means "Tools." Please feel free to laugh hysterically now.

Alex

I really respected this guy, and I didn't want him to think less of me. I wanted to lie about my situation to Steven to save face. I didn't want to admit I was struggling with technology (again). I didn't want him to think I didn't have my s#$% together. I didn't want to feel awkward. I held my breath and felt the warm, very familiar flush of awkward anxiety rush over me.

I hit send.

He wrote, almost immediately, the best response I could've asked for. He *was* apparently laughing, told me it was OK, and said we could reschedule once I got it all figured out. And then he asked if he could use my message in his work sometime.

He ended his message with: *"We're all in the same leaky boat when it comes to technology."*

Well isn't that the truth?

And, I'd like to take that truth a step farther and add my own twist.

We're all in the same leaky *minivan,* traveling on the road of life.

If you and I are going to lead a life where we are confident in ourselves, we've got to own our awkward moments. We have to stop covering up our awkwardness with little white lies that we think don't mean much at the time. We must stop pretending we weren't singing at the top of our lungs, putting on mascara, or talking to ourselves at the stoplight. When we aren't honest about what's really going on, not only are we not being our truest selves, but we're blocking the one thing we need most in an awkward moment.

Which is to know we aren't alone.

P.S.
You and I are in same leaky, awkward minivan called "life," and we're on the road together. Why not be confident in the fact that we don't have all the answers, aren't always put together, and honestly, we're just hanging on for dear life sometimes?

What's in a name?

"If you don't fall down, you aren't trying hard enough."

–Tenley Albright, Figure Skater, Polio Survivor,
Surgeon, Cancer Researcher[15]

I was getting ready to start a workshop on delivering exceptional customer care. Exceptional customer care, mind you, is critically important to this story. I'd been doing individual client work with the company—coaching the vice president, as well as helping to prepare the series of educational seminars for the entire staff. I'd had limited but still significant interactions with the entire executive team, including the president of the company. He wanted to kick off the day by saying a few words, introducing me to the group, and then I would take over.

So, that he did. He said a few words about how excited he was to have me there, how much everyone was going to learn, and why it was important to the company as a whole. He ended by giving me a nice, warm introduction.

And I thanked him by name.

It just didn't happen to be *his* name.

It's still hard for me not to twitch when I think about it.

I got his name wrong.

I got the company president's name wrong in front of the entire staff. I called him by the wrong name in front of all of his people. *All of them.* No one missed that day. Nope, not a single soul. All forty-five of them heard me call their president by the wrong name.

And, to make things even worse, the name I *did* call him was the name of the vice president of the company. The vice president he didn't like very much. Not much at all. And everyone knew it.

You could have heard a pin drop. Time slowed just a bit as I watched his face go from mildly pleasant to mostly horrified. I imagine my face looked completely horrified. He was mid-stride, walking away from his spot in the front of the room to his seat in the back. He stopped and quickly snapped back, "You mean Steve." (Not his real name.)

The awkwardness of the moment hung in the air like a thick fog. The employees were looking at Steve, they were looking at me, and in that moment, we were all wondering what was going to happen next. In reality, I wanted to pretend it didn't happen. I wanted to run. I wanted to do anything but stand there wondering what to do. Still stuck in my own feelings of horror, I uttered a sort of weird half-laugh, half-scream, and then immediately threw my arms out as wide as I could and said in an overly loud, exaggerated voice:

"And that, ladies and gentlemen, is why we're here—to make sure you don't make a mistake like I just did, calling a client by the wrong name."

It was just awkward enough to break the tension.

The employees laughed, and while I could have been imagining it, I think I saw "Steve" crack just a tiny bit of a smile at my antics. I made sure to thank him appropriately for his warm welcome and the opportunity to spend time with his employees.

Now hear me out on this one. I am not supporting the idea that you go into situations unprepared or that it's OK to forget people's names. Neither of these are OK. What I *am* pointing out here is that, despite our best efforts and often in the most inopportune moments, we are, from time to time, going to do something epically awkward like forget someone's name. Someone important. It's awkward when it happens, and, many times, it's even more awkward to try to recover. But awkwardness is going to happen, and it isn't always going to be easy to deal with. In situations like this one, you might find yourself, like me, choosing more awkwardness to combat the discomfort you've already created. That's OK. Embrace awkward every time you can, every way you can. You'll walk away with more confidence, knowing you can handle a similar situation better the next time around, and you'll save yourself the pain of having to make up for the awkwardness later.

P.S.

Think of it like this: forgetting someone else's name is awkward. Forgetting your own name is even worse. You can come back from forgetting someone else's name. I'm not sure you get to come back from forgetting your own.

You're making things awkward

"It's infinitely more rewarding to understand than to be right — even if that means changing your mind about a topic, an ideology, or above all, yourself."
–Maria Popova, Blogger, Marketer, Modern-Day Philosopher[16]

Awkwardness is hard enough when it happens to us by accident, like tripping over an imaginary rock on the sidewalk, waving at a random stranger who isn't waving at you, or losing control over bodily functions in front of people we don't know very well. But it's even worse when we manifest our own awkwardness. When we start thinking about being awkward, we often react accordingly when there wasn't a need for awkwardness in the first place. Like when we start worrying that we're going to say something dumb in front a new friend or coworker … and then we do. Or when we're worried about looking uncomfortable and we get nervous, and next thing you know, we're creating all sorts of weird moments.

We can make awkwardness come out of thin air simply by spending too much time in our heads. Talk about a confidence killer. Why the heck do we do this? Unfortunately, it's part of our human condition. Somewhere along the line, when we developed self-awareness and awareness of others, we also developed the skills of overthinking, overanalyzing, and overreacting. This can lead to taking situations that are otherwise completely normal and filling them with all kinds of weird and unnecessary awkwardness. Sometimes, it's just temporary; sometimes it's more permanent. Many times, it stifles who we are, how we act, and how we're perceived by others. It can even cause us to quit relationships or activities we love. In other words, sometimes when we're driving along the road of life, without any assistance or guidance from other people, we steer ourselves head-on into a big old pile-up of human awkwardness.

Let me give you an example. I was 99.9 percent sure I was going to quit my gym. Lots of folks quit their gyms every day, and maybe you're not quite the gym rat I am, so let me explain why this matters so much. My gym is my happy place. My home away from home. The place where I go to work off all the stress of the day, hang with some of my favorite people, and pretend I'm an elite-level athlete (hey, this is a book on confidence—a gal can dream, can't she?). Basically, I can't imagine my life without my gym. If push came to shove and it came down to giving up food or the gym, I'd probably choose giving up food. Anyway, not long ago, I was 99.9 percent sure I was going to quit my gym, and I was going to quit because of Bryn, the guy who owns the gym. The guy who's been my coach for the last six years. Yep, he was the problem. (Don't worry, he knows this story.)

I can't tell you exactly how it started. Maybe it was a combination of a bad day, an awkward interaction with him, or just a bout of insecurity—I'm not totally sure, but somehow or another, I got the idea in my head that Bryn didn't like me very much. I had zero evidence to prove this theory, so I found myself looking for reasons to confirm my new belief.

I found myself thinking things like:

"He didn't say hi when I walked in ... did he even see me?"

"He seems so standoffish today."

"I know that 'Bryn face' was directed at me." (Note that "Bryn face" is known throughout the gym as an unwanted expression that indicates your form is bad—again.)

The more I looked for it, the more I noticed the awkwardness that I believed was happening between Bryn and me. Before I realized it, my behavior toward Bryn started to change. I kept my big, cheesy grin and silly antics to myself. I stopped asking him questions because it just felt too awkward. Eventually, I found myself avoiding classes he taught and contemplated switching gyms. *That'll show him, right?*

This went on for a while. I looked at other gyms, talked about it with my husband and some of my friends. I just couldn't shake the awkwardness that I felt around him. I didn't want to leave, but it was becoming almost unbearable to be in the gym. I felt so awkward.

Then his coaching schedule changed and, one morning, I ended up in his five o'clock CrossFit class. I remember thinking, *I don't want to give up this class just because he's here.* (You can question my early morning ways another time.) I remember waking up kind of antsy, because I knew I was going to be in *his* class. We hadn't seen each other in a while, so it was bound to be awkward.

I walked in the door, and Bryn greeted me with a big smile and asked how things had been going. *Hmm ... that's nice,* I thought, and I relaxed a little. Class that day was great; Bryn coached me, cheered me on, and all seemed OK. Things seemed different. I thought, *Well, we'll see if this continues.*

And it did. It didn't take long before I was enjoying his classes again, asking questions, and dancing around like I do. When I'm having fun, it shows. *Man,* I thought, *Bryn's so much better! He's smiling and chatty. This is great!* The awkwardness that had been so acute before seemed to be disappearing. I wanted to know why.

So, I decided to ask him, "What's different about you?" I completely caught him off guard. Looking back, that must have felt super awkward to him. He was polite and said something about fewer pressures at home, new coaches on staff to help, etc. Good enough answer, but it didn't explain why things felt so different to me.

Time to insert a facepalm emoji here. There wasn't anything different about Bryn. Bryn was still Bryn. The only thing that has made our relationship awkward was me. Bryn was blissfully unaware of the awkward thoughts I had rolling around in my head. Shocking, I know. He was busy doing his thing. I was the one making it awkward.

Had I asked Bryn to confirm or deny my thoughts before I launched into all of my awkward behavior?

No.

I believed the story in my head, and I started searching for reasons to believe it was true.

You've probably had something like this happen to you. Like when you start believing your boss thinks you stink at your job, and you start listing all the ways you think you stink to confirm your faulty belief. Or when you're doubtful about a decision you made as a mom, and the next thing you know, you're ranting to your sister about all the ways you're a bad mom. Or maybe when you look in the mirror and tell yourself you're ugly, and then you create a laundry list of all the reasons why that's true. The official name for this effect is *confirmation bias*—what we look for, we find. In this case, I was looking for an awkward relationship with Bryn, and by doing so, I created it. I made things awkward when they weren't really awkward at all. I was self-sabotaging my confidence in my relationship with Bryn, and I bet you've done something like this too.

My friend, sometimes we are awkward, and we've got to own that. Sometimes, though, as in this story with Bryn, we need to question whether or not what we're thinking is something we should really believe. Our thoughts and our feelings aren't necessarily facts. So before we let them run amok, causing us to question our confidence, it's a good idea to fact-check them first. In this case, what I should have done right away was ask Bryn if something was up between us and then believed his answer. You can do that, too, in your relationships. Or if it's a thought you're having about yourself—like, "Ugh, I'm so ugly" or "I suck at my job!"—stop yourself in the moment and ask, "Is that really true?" And answer honestly. My guess is, you're self-sabotaging. Stop it right there and remind yourself of things you do that make you feel confident. Name three things that make you feel confident about your looks. Name three things that make you feel confident about your work, or three things that make you feel confident about your relationship. You'll immediately refocus and remember that you deserve to feel confident, exactly as you are.

P.S.
What you look for, you will find.
Always look for confidence.

Remember: When someone catches you singing
at a stoplight, smile and wave!

ANSWER THE FOLLOWING QUESTIONS

1. Were you awkward today? How did it keep you from feeling or being confident? In hindsight, what would you do differently?
2. What do you need to do to make peace with the fact that you're going to have awkward moments?
3. How will you feel if you choose to own your awkward moments rather than try to hide them?
4. How much more confident will you be if you choose to focus on moving past your awkward moments instead of dwelling on them?
5. How will your life improve if you choose to be confident and laugh at your awkward moments?

CHAPTER FOUR

ROAD RULE 4: IT'S OK TO STOP
AND ASK FOR DIRECTIONS.

*"Good judgment, with experience, has taught some to measure by sight;
but the majority need definite guides."*

–FANNIE FARMER, CULINARY PIONEER,
TEEN STROKE SURVIVOR, COOKING SCHOOL PRINCIPAL[17]

Introduction

Being confident is a journey. A road trip with no final destination, only stops along the way. You're going to hit potholes, have a few fender benders, and most likely, experience a few epic crashes. You're going to change vehicles, get new tires, and sometimes you might even end up as a passenger instead of the driver. You're going to need help, lots of it.

There will be many times when you're going to need other people to help get you unstuck, restarted, refueled, and repaired. When I talk about asking for help, I'm talking about getting real about the fact that you and I don't, won't, and cannot possibly ever have it all figured out. We need other people to help us along the way.

But if we're honest with ourselves, asking for help is one of the hardest things in the world to do. Admitting to yourself and to others that you don't have it all figured out, don't know where to look, or that you're lost can feel awful. You and I live in a world where asking for help is oftentimes viewed as a weakness, that we're supposed to, as adults, have it "all figured out." You might tell yourself it's not OK to ask for help because you don't want to burden someone with your problems. Or you don't want to ask because, "Well, other people have it so much tougher than I do." Maybe you don't ask because you're afraid of being rejected, or worse, you've been rejected before when you've asked. There's the fear that if you ask for help, you'll become dependent on someone, and you value your independence. Maybe you grew up with parents who struggled to ask for help, so you didn't have good role models when it comes to seeking support from other people. And what happens if you ask for help and the other person expects something in return? Something you can't or don't want to give? Isn't it just easier to pick up a book or do a quick online search to figure things out? I haven't checked, but there's probably a YouTube video out there that promises something like "Find Confidence in Seven Minutes." If only it were that simple.

Sometimes we get annoyed by people who ask for "too much" help. The coworker who just can't seem to figure things out, the friend who comes to you repeatedly with the same problems but doesn't heed your advice or suggestions. If you're a parent, sometimes it's your kids. "I've explained this to them a thousand times," you might think. "Why aren't they getting it?" If you're married, you might get annoyed by your spouse. "Why can't they just figure it out?" Maybe you don't want to become *that person,* so you avoid asking for help because you know how annoying it is.

For the sake of the argument, I'm going to assume that you err on the side of not asking for help more often than not. If that's true, then you'll find the stories that follow in this next chapter helpful. Because what I've learned on my own minivan journey of life is that asking for help is *essential*. We need other people to help us see who we are and who we're not. We need other people to call when we're struggling to make decisions, when we're at our wit's end, when we're unsure, lost, or just stuck. Your asks could be as simple as, "Hey, would you come over and take a look at this to see if I've made any spelling errors?" Or as complex and emotional as, "Can you help me? I just lost my job." How much, how often, and who you ask for help will vary depending on your circumstances and your personality. But there are no right or wrong answers.

Some asks will be easy; some will be mind-numbingly hard. That's why I want to share these stories with you. I want to encourage you to ask—and keep asking—for help along the way. I want to remind you that it's not just OK to ask for help, it's essential. I want to encourage you to ask for help even when it makes you feel silly or dumb. I want to encourage you to ask for help even when it's crazy hard, and you're scared to do it. I want to encourage you to ask for help even when your pride is screaming at you, "I can do it on my own, and I should do it on my own. I'm an adult, for goodness' sake!" I want you to know that asking for help shows you're confident in what you know *and* what you don't know. No one knows everything. *No one.*

We aren't meant to go it alone on the road of life. Being yourself— truly yourself—requires you to acknowledge that you don't and won't have it all figured it out. I'm here to remind you that asking for help isn't a weakness. It's a sign of strength. The beauty of asking for help is that sometimes—many times—the act alone will increase your confidence, and isn't that what we're going for?

P.S.
Some of the best relationships I've formed have
come as a result of reaching out for help.

What do you do when you're literally stuck?

*"'Thank you' is the best prayer that anyone could say. I say that one a lot.
'Thank you' expresses extreme gratitude, humility, understanding."*

–ALICE WALKER, NOVELIST, POET, SOCIAL ACTIVIST[18]

You might think that after five and half years of driving a minivan, a person would be exceptionally good at it. You might think that after countless experiences taking a van across the country to multiple cities both large and small, a person would be accustomed to situating their minivan in tight spaces, backing out of long and short driveways, and they might even be comfortable with the occasional parallel parking challenge. You might think that such a person would be undaunted by most of the everyday challenges that come with driving and parking a larger vehicle. I'm sure that for many, many people—possibly even you—these things are true. However, in my case, you would be wrong. Dead wrong. I'm not good at any of it. Not good at all. *Bad* is a word that comes to mind. Dangerous—not really—I mean, unless you're a fire hydrant or a garage door (my van and I have had a few exceptionally spectacular run-ins with these two characters, which didn't end well—not for them or my pocketbook).

I am, at best, a mediocre minivan driver. *Sigh*. I do my very best to avoid all sorts of situations that might get me into trouble with the van, like parallel parking, backing out of long driveways, and navigating narrow streets, so I don't embarrass myself or anyone else with my lack of minivan-driving prowess. However, from time to time, I find myself in the uncomfortable position of having to deal with what, for most people, are no-big-deal situations with the van. Case in point, the last time I parked on a narrow street in Indianapolis.

Here's what happened: I drove downtown to meet a client. Now, you understand that for many of us who live outside the city, it's considered a big deal to have to drive downtown. Some of us consider it a *major* inconvenience to make the *epically long trek to the big city*. I've traveled enough to know we have it ridiculously good here when it comes to driving. We're nothing like Chicago, New York City, or LA. But let's face it, the things we like to complain about as humans are all relative to our personal situations. Thus, driving to downtown Indianapolis is a pain for those of us who don't live close (i.e., in the city itself).

Anyway, I'd driven downtown to a local coffee shop that I hadn't been to before. I wasn't sure of the parking situation and I was relieved to see there was open, angled, meter parking on the street in front of the shop. I found a spot close to the door, walked in, ordered a flat white, and met my client.

After our meeting was over and we'd thrown our coffee cups away, I headed out the front door. The street where my van was parked was narrow. Very narrow. I looked up and saw that a food service semi had parked right behind my van and the other cars in front of the shop. The space between his truck and my van seemed tight—too tight for my tastes and my questionable ability to steer the van in the direction I want it to go when I'm backing it up. I thought to myself, *Oh great, how long am I going to have to wait for that guy to move his truck?* I looked around but didn't see the driver anywhere. Not a good sign. I hopped in my van, checked messages on my phone, and took a look at the truck in my rearview mirror. *Hmm.* How long do I wait? *Not long,* I thought. *I'm starving.* Stuck plus hungry isn't a great combo for me.

I looked around again. No movement. I looked to my left and saw an empty Honda Civic. I looked to my right and saw a Koorsen service truck with the driver still inside, smoking a cigarette. *Hmm.* Sometimes—a.k.a. more often than not—my pride gets the best of me. I didn't want the service guy to my right to see me a.) sitting in my van waiting, looking lost and confused, or b.) attempting to back up the van and hitting the truck behind us. Nope. That would stink. So I reminded myself that I am a very capable person, a very intelligent person who by all means can and should back up her van, grab some lunch, and head home.

I put the van in reverse, checked my mirror, and whispered to myself, "I can do this." I ever so slowly started to back up, attempting to turn the steering wheel sharply enough to angle the van in just the right position so I could easily get out of my parking spot. I checked my side mirrors—all good there. I continued inching my way out of the spot and watching as I moved the van closer and closer toward the truck. *It's so close,* I thought, and I inched just a bit more, bracing myself for a thud. I pushed just a few more fractions of an inch, but I could tell I wasn't going to make it. I didn't feel like I could make it. I put the van in park, hopped out, and walked around to the back of the van. It looked like there was a couple of feet more I could go, but in my mind, the van was still too crooked to make it work. I got back in and pulled the van into the spot.

Ugh.

Why does driving have to be so hard?

I tried again and failed, repeating my movements almost exactly. I tried again, no luck. I tried again and again, and at some point, I lost count and began to worry. Frustrated, hungry, and now convinced I would spend the rest of my day trapped by a truck, I wondered how long I could survive on the stale crackers from Wendy's in the glove compartment. Dramatic? Perhaps.

I looked left. The Honda Civic was still next to me, empty. I looked right. The Koorsen service truck was still there too, and the driver was still inside.

Oh, good Lord, I thought.

This guy saw me backing in and out like a fool. I wasn't going to die of starvation after all. I was going to die of embarrassment. *Smooth move, Alex—way to show off your expert driving skills.*

Somewhere in the deep recesses of my mind, an idea emerged: *You know, Alex, you could just ask the guy for help. I mean, after all, he drives a service truck—he's probably good at getting in and out of tight spaces.*

My not-so-rational mind answered quickly: *Nope. Can't do it. Can't do it because the guy probably already saw me making a fool of myself trying to pull out, and he's going to think I'm nutso for asking. Not a chance. Nope. Plus, he's probably a murderer. Yup, he's gotta be a murderer, and I'm not about to become a news headline today. Not. Going. To. Happen.*

I sat there mentally willing the driver of the truck to come out of the building to no avail. My stomach grumbled. I watched a few minutes tick by on the dashboard clock. It was dumb to just keep sitting here. I either needed to ask for help or try again to back out. Given that I'd tried the latter with zero success, asking for help was, without a doubt, my best option. I started talking to myself again: *OK, Alex, pull it together. Just knock on the guy's window and ask him to pull the van out of the spot. He's not going to steal the van. He's not going to murder you in broad daylight in front of a busy building. The dude is probably just sitting there waiting for his next assignment to come in from dispatch.*

I opened up my door, walked around the back of the van over to his truck, and knocked on the window. Mr. Koorsen Service Man looked over with a mildly surprised expression. He rolled down his window, and before he could start talking, I did.

"Uh, hi there. Sorry to bother you and all, but I noticed you here, and, well, um, I'm having trouble getting my van out because of the big truck behind us, and I was wondering if you, um, might be willing to help me?"

After what felt like an hour of awkward silence, but was really probably a second or two, he said, "Sure. Ya want me to stand behind ya and tell ya where to go?"

Oh, Mr. Koorsen Service Man, you don't understand, do you? You really didn't see me pulling in and out time after time? If you had, you wouldn't be willing to risk your life in such a way.

"Uh, um, well, actually, if I just give you the keys, would you, you know, just kinda pull it out for me? I mean, it would probably be easier that way." *And your life would be in much, much less danger.*

He looked down at his phone and then back up at me and said, "You want me to pull it out for you? Uh ... ok, I guess I can do that." He set his phone in a cup holder, and I backed up so he could open the door.

As he got out and I started walking him to the driver's side of the van, I kind of half-handed, half-threw my keys at him, all while mumbling, "Thanks so much. I really appreciate this. I know you're busy, but it's such a huge help."

He opened up the driver's-side door and moved the seat back so he could sit down. I told him I'd stay out and watch, you know, just in case he needed help. (Or if he was in fact a murderer who had just been waiting for the opportunity to pounce on some hopelessly challenged minivan driver.) He started the van, threw it into reverse, and backed it out in no less than fifteen seconds.

He said, "There ya go!"

I thanked him again, telling him how silly I felt for asking and how much I appreciated his willingness to help a stranger out.

He said, "Of course. My wife can't back up her van when it's in a tight spot either, so I do this kinda thing all the time. I mean, she's dung it on the side of the garage and all kinds of stuff. I was happy to help ya, Miss."

I shook his hand, thanked him again, and hopped back into the van.

I was saved, and my pride, while bruised, was still intact. I drove off, wishing I'd asked him sooner. It would have been way easier and much less stressful. Lesson learned the hard way that day: *It's OK to ask for help. Always has been, always will be.*

Is it a silly story to share with you? Perhaps. How does it relate to confidence? Let me tell you. I knew with a fair amount of confidence that I wasn't going to be able to back up my van to get it out of the spot. I knew my previous driving mistakes and bumbles in the van well enough to know that there was a good chance I was going to do something dumb, hit somebody, and/or at a minimum stress myself out completely by trying to do it. I knew on that day what my strengths were and what they were not. Could I have eventually made it? Sure. But was there an easier, faster, and safer way? Absolutely. Looking back, I could have, should have, and still wish I had asked the driver next to me sooner. I wish I had owned that I have strengths and weakness, like everyone else, and that I can't be good at everything. Confidence isn't having it all figured out—it's about knowing yourself well and not letting your pride get in the way of moving through life smoothly.

You know what your strengths and weaknesses are. You know what you're good at and what you're not. You know what you want to learn and what you'd prefer not to. You know that you can't know it all, do it all, or be it all. Be confident in that knowledge. When you're confident in what you don't know, it makes it easier to reach out for help. And it will save you a lot of time, energy, and money. Acknowledging your weakness also comes with the extra bonus of making someone else feel good because they got to do something helpful. Most people like that feeling—they simply need to be asked.

Asking for help, even with the "silly" stuff, isn't a sign of weakness; it's a sign of confidence. Be confident about what you don't know and ask for help.

P.S.

After that day, I realized I hadn't even bothered to ask for the guy's name. *Ugh.* I decided to write a post and tag Koorsen so they'd know what a wonderful employee they have in that driver who helped me. I've included it below because I'm pretty proud of it, and I think you'll appreciate the message.

Dear Koorsen Service Man,

You saved my day yesterday. You see, my minivan and I, we have a complicated relationship. We love each other for all the obvious reasons. But we struggle with tight spaces, parking, garages ... don't even mention the word 'parallel' around her.
Yesterday we were STUCK.
There we were, right by Quills on 9th in Indianapolis. I thought I'd chosen a metered spot well, but I hadn't anticipated the delivery truck that would park itself behind me, putting me in the awkward spot of trying to pull out with what in my mind was absolutely ZERO room.
We struggled, my minivan and I, pulling in and out, trying hard to adjust my angle to get it just right so I could slip away.

*But alas, my fear of ramming my sweet ride
into the back of that service truck kept me from
pulling out, and I worried that I'd be stuck in that
metered spot for the rest of the day.*

*Then I saw you, Mr. Koorsen man, in the spot
next to me.*

*I'm sure I surprised you when I jumped out of
my van and knocked on your window.*

*I asked if you'd help me back out ... actually, if
you'd just do it for me. You said 'yes' and hopped
in and got me set straight so I could get on with
my day.*

*I was so relieved and rushing on my way,
I didn't even get your name. I'm sorry about
that. We're not going to save the world in a day.
However, if we're open and willing to help, we can
save someone else's day.*

Thank you, Mr. Koorsen Man, for saving mine.

Alex

Teenager + Shopping = Angst

"Create 'Team You.'"

–KELLY HOLMES, OLYMPIC RUNNER,
MILITARY VET, MENTAL HEALTH ADVOCATE[19]

Dress shopping with your daughter is supposed to be a rite of passage as a mom. At least, that's how I've always pictured it. I'd dreamed about taking my daughter to get a dress for her first dance. I'd pictured us strolling through the aisles of department stores, giggling and laughing. I imagined her walking out of the dressing room in all sorts of dresses, each one better than the last. We'd decide on the blue one—no wait, the red one. We'd buy both because, well, we'd have to see them in the daylight to truly decide. We'd go out for a celebratory dinner afterward where she would glow with anticipation of her very first dance. So when it came time to take Carmen dress shopping for her junior high school winter dance, I was over-the-moon excited.

It was a feeling that lasted about fifteen seconds before she informed me that we'd be going with a group of her friends and their moms. *OK*, I thought. *This doesn't have to ruin the dream— shopping with friends is fun. This will be great.*

We made plans with her girlfriends to meet up at JCPenny to begin our shopping extravaganza. Now, if you've ever spent time with a group of junior high school girls, you know how this goes. They all swarm together and take off as far ahead of you as humanly possible so as not to be seen with an adult. They roam around aimlessly, squeaking, squealing, and laughing hysterically at things that only *they* think are funny. They'll return to the adult or adults only when needed for decision-making, money, and/or transportation to the next location where they can once again pretend that they are old enough to get there on their own. Not exactly the mother-daughter bonding experience I had hoped for, but she's a teenager—I remember those days—so I gave her some space and I hung back with the other moms.

After about ten minutes of aimless wandering, we ended up in the junior's section where the girls found dresses of all sorts to try on. They grabbed handfuls each and headed off into the dressing room. The girls took turns coming out and parading around in their dresses—some perfectly appropriate, others no mother would ever let her daughter wear out of the dressing room. Carmen came out in a dress that clearly didn't work, so she went back in and tried again. And again. And again. Not a single dress fit or complemented her figure or her preferences. I tried to help, but all I got was pushback.

I watched as her other friends picked out dresses that they loved. I watched her try on what was for real a mother-of-the-bride dress. I wanted her so badly to find a dress that made her feel good, that made her feel confident in her own skin. Every time she walked out in something that didn't work, I knew my face was betraying me, that she could see the disappointment in my eyes. *Way to go, Mom,* I told myself. *Way to make this all about you.*

I wanted to be the cool mom, the one who was easy to turn to in situations like these. But I wasn't. It was definitely not the Hallmark movie experience I'd hoped for. I wanted to cry. I felt like I had failed my daughter. If you're a mom, you get it, right? There's nothing worse than feeling like you've let your kid down, that you weren't able to help when your kid needed it.

When it was time to go, she still hadn't found a dress. To make matters worse, I wasn't going to be able to take her out again because a.) it was her weekend with her dad, and b.) I had work obligations. She needed the dress ASAP for the following weekend, and she wanted it ASAP. Now, I know we can't always give our kids what they want ASAP, but if you're a mom, you know that disappointing your kid is tough. What the heck was I going to do? I wanted her to have a dress like the rest of her friends, but I was out of time, out of luck, and out of options. Unless I was willing to ask for help.

Asking for help as a mom is hard. I mean, aren't we supposed to be able to do it all? Mom guilt over not being able to do, be, and say all the right things at the right times is *real*. It's a real pain in the butt. I experience ridiculous amounts of mom guilt at times because Carmen is my only biological kiddo (I've got step-kids and other kids in my extended family whom I adore, but it's different). Things like dress shopping for the first time take on an extra significance for me. Every first is also a last—there's no other kiddo who will go through the same things. I wanted to be the one who was with her when she found *the dress*. But it wasn't going to happen, not without major alterations to the schedule. It wasn't my weekend with her; it was her daddy's. I'd have to rework all kinds of stuff to make up time. I'd be inconveniencing more than just myself, and that wasn't fair. I wanted Carmen to have her dress like the rest of her friends, and that meant I was going to have to ask for help.

I called Jen, Carmen's stepmom, and filled her in on our unsuccessful shopping trip. Jen and I are close—we've been close for a long time. That's the stuff of a different van ride, a different book, a great story I'll have to tell you later. Just know for now that when I picked up the phone and said, "Jen, I need your help," she one hundred percent understood how hard that was for me to do as a mom. She knew I had wanted that extra special dress-shopping experience with Carmen, and she knew that asking another mom to take over had taken a lot of guts—a lot of confidence.

I was confident Jen was going to be able to help, and I was confident I was making the right decision for Carmen. And I was right. Jen and Carmen went shopping the next morning, and they found a dress my kiddo loved. Carmen called to tell me all about it; she sent me pictures, she looked and sounded happy. She went to the dance feeling beautiful. What more could a mom ask for?

I strive to teach Carmen to surround herself with other strong women and to lean into them when she needs them. I couldn't help her find a dress, but I gave her something that will outlast even a couture gown: I showed her how to reach out and ask for help when she needs it.

Parenting is hard. Asking for help as a parent is especially hard. You want to be everything to your kids. You want to show them you are the hero they already believe you are. You want to show them you're invincible, that you've always got their backs, and that you'd do anything for them. But one of the best things you can do for your kids is to show them you *can't* do everything for them. One of the best things you can do for your kids and for yourself is remember that it's OK to ask for help. Asking for help isn't a sign of weakness. *It's a sign of confidence.* Being confident doesn't require you to have all the right answers or to do everything on your own. True confidence comes from knowing your limits and asking for help when you need it.

P.S.

A confident woman knows not only what she's good at but where she falls short, and she's not afraid to ask another woman for help when she needs it.

Google doesn't have all the answers

"From what I've seen, it isn't so much the act of asking that paralyzes us—it's what lies beneath: the fear of being vulnerable, the fear of rejection, the fear of looking needy or weak. The fear of being seen as a burdensome member of the community instead of a productive one. It points, fundamentally, to our separation from one another."

–AMANDA PALMER, AUTHOR OF THE ART OF ASKING[20]

If my internet sources are correct, Google receives over 63,000 searches per second, every day.[21]

That adds up to over two trillion searches per year. I didn't make it far enough in math to know how many zeros you need to get to a trillion. I'd have to do a Google search to find out. But that's a lot of zeros and a lot searches.

So. Many. Searches.

I'm a huge fan of Google. I use Google all the time. I honestly have a hard time remembering what life was like before Google existed. Google has become, for many of us, our first go-to whenever we need something. An answer, an idea, inspiration, or help. And while it's been a tremendously huge help to all of us, there's also a downside. One I'm sure Google doesn't want you to know about.One I'm sure you're aware of on some level.

Google doesn't have all the answers.

Despite what the great Google gods might have us believe, despite what you encounter on a daily basis, despite what you might want to believe deep down in your heart (because it's way easier to ask Google sometimes than it is to ask another person), even Google can be stumped. I know this first-hand because I did it. I stumped Google. Google doesn't have all the answers.

Let me tell you about it. At the very beginning when I started my company, Practically Speaking, I didn't have much, and by not having much, I mean I had almost zero dollars in my bank account and I was working off a card table. This was around month two—I had exactly two clients, and I knew if I was ever going to make my business work, I was going to need a website. However, I knew website designers were pricey, and I didn't have enough in my budget to pay someone to do the work. I mean, let's be serious here, I didn't have money to pay myself, let alone anyone else. I had barely paid for my start-up costs and my laptop. I could've gone into debt, but I was nowhere near that level of commitment yet. So, I decided I'd just have to build a website myself.

Oh boy. Me, the Skype-in-Arabic girl. Me, the Gen-Xer who has a perilous, dare I say *dangerous,* relationship with technology. I was going to build my own website. And I believed it was going to be great!

Oh, naive, naive Alex. I kind of wish I could go back and give that version of me a big old hug and tell her to back away from the computer.

I already had a Google G Suite account, which boasted the capability of website design included in the low, low price of $9.99 per month, which I was already paying for my email. Sweet G Suite. I was in luck! (Or at least I thought I was. I was definitely wrong.) I purchased an uninspiring domain name, and I was on my way to having my very own website. Designed by me.

I spent hours, days actually—OK, two weeks—working on the darn thing. By the time I'd finished, I'd managed to create three whole pages plus the home page, which proudly displayed my first logo that looked kind of like the *Star Wars* logo, except it was black and red. Each page was created with—I'm almost ashamed to tell you—black-and-white clip art of people in business suits ... because clip art is free. Each of the pages had terribly written copy that read like an '80s advertisement for professional speaking services. Each with a font that I'm not even sure you can find anymore and, unfortunately, each of the pages were also woefully disconnected from the home page.

I tried to fix the issue myself, I promise. I searched and read the help pages, trying to figure out why I couldn't get them to link. I called the Google helpline and thought I'd come up with a solution with the expert on the other end, but for some reason (possibly user failure?), I couldn't get the darn thing to work.

I had succeeded in building a website, succeeded through sheer power of will, lots and lots of coffee, and many, many expletives muttered under my breath. Forgive me, I tried, but technology brings out my dark side. I couldn't get it to work right. So I called Google again.

Because Google has all the answers, doesn't it?

I called, and I got Ivan. I sort of wondered for about half a second if Ivan was his real name, but it didn't matter. I'd come this far, I'd worked so hard, I would've called him Sir Silly Pants McGee if he wanted me to. I did not care. I just wanted my little-website-that-almost-could to work.

I described the issue to Ivan, who promptly told me I'd have to wait while he investigated. Not ideal but not a surprise either. This wasn't my first call center rodeo. Ivan came back on the line and asked a few more questions. I did my best to answer in my broken technology speak. He asked me to hold again.

We repeated this process about four times, with only slight variations. A keystroke here, a search there, some information required for further investigation. The call went on for an hour, then an hour and fifteen minutes, then ninety minutes eventually passed. We still had no solution.

Ivan put me on hold again, and I thought I was going to lose my mind. *Why does everything have to be so hard?* I asked the elevator music playing in the background. *Isn't technology supposed to make my life easier?*

I don't know how long it was before Ivan popped back on the line. But I can still hear him: "Uh, Mrs. Perry, there isn't a solution to your problem."

I laughed out loud because, surely, this had to be a joke. I didn't just spend weeks working on a website and hours on the phone, trying to get it to work, only to be told that there was no solution. Was my issue *that* crazy?

I said, "What do you mean? What do I need to do to fix the problem?" Poor Ivan, he would have done well to just hang up, pretending we'd lost the connection.

Ivan said, "I don't know. I don't know how to fix your problem."

I thought, *This cannot be real. This cannot possibly be real. I am talking to the greatest power on the internet (or at least a representative of the greatest power on the internet), and you're telling me you don't know?!*

I was exhausted. I was frustrated. And I was defeated. My issue really was that crazy. Poor Ivan. I do my best to be kind to people, especially people who work in the service industry. Call center representatives have a hard gig. Especially when they've got to deal with someone like me who has lost their marbles.

But all of the pent-up stress and anxiety I'd had over attempting to build my own website, the stress of trying to start a business from scratch, the stress of not knowing how on Earth I was ever going to make it all happen came out. I became unhinged.

I yelled—no, I screamed—into the phone.

"BUT YOU'RE GOOGLE! YOU'RE SUPPOSED TO HAVE ALL THE ANSWERS!"

Poor Ivan.

He stammered back, "I'm sorry, Miss. I just don't know how to help you."

I've sort of blanked out the rest of what I said to him. I have no doubt it went something along the lines of describing just how ticked off I was, how hard I had worked, and how I just couldn't believe a business like Google wouldn't know the solution to a problem with their very own product. I have no doubt I sounded exactly like a disappointed, disapproving mom.

Ivan listened patiently, and after who knows how long, I hung up, put my head down on the table, and cried. My made-from-scratch website really wasn't going to work, which was a good thing in the end because I don't think even *I* could have taken myself seriously with all of that clip art.

In the end, I ended up having a lot of help with my website. I had a designer and her staff assist me step-by-step through the process, and I had lots of input from family and friends. I learned that doing it with the help of others was a much better idea than doing it on my own. I learned to ask for help and to keep asking until I got the answers I needed.

So what's the point—why does this matter to you? What does it have to do with being confident? I mean, you're probably not in the midst of building a website (but if you are and need moral support, please feel free to call me). It matters because I couldn't sing the praises of asking for help without pointing out that no one, not even Google, has *all* of the answers.

It's easy to fall prey to the idea that the quick and easy answers are right at our fingertips. We're led to believe that a Google search can and will be the answer to our problems—that a Facebook or Instagram post will instantly yield solutions. And it's true, social media and Google are in fact great in many circumstances, like when you need to know what type of air filter to buy for your van, or where the nearest sushi place is, or whether or not your local gas station sells Cheetos. Google is probably great for building a website if you're techy (or better at it than I am).

But I'm talking about something bigger here. I mean it when I say that Google *really* doesn't have all the answers you're looking for to some of the bigger questions in life. Like:

- "How can I feel confident in my own skin?"
- "What's my ultimate life purpose?"
- Or, "Why can't I just be happy?"

You might get ideas, but the real answers come from asking other people how they've done it, what's helped them, and from doing the work on your own—like reading a helpful book—to figure it out. It's OK to ask these questions again and again with different people in different circumstances, and the more the merrier. Sure, it might feel weird at first, but I promise you the more you do it, the more confident you'll be in asking for help as you figure out the big stuff. And maybe, just maybe, you'll be more confident in figuring yourself out too.

P.S.
If you run into a guy named Ivan from Google,
tell him I'm sorry for yelling at him.

Remember: It's OK to stop and ask for directions.

ANSWER THE FOLLOWING QUESTIONS

1. Who have you asked for help today? How did it make you feel?
2. What would make it easier for you to ask for help?
3. When was a time you needed to ask for help but didn't? Why did you hesitate?
4. How would your circumstances improve if you had chosen/could choose to ask for help (even when it's hard)?
5. Who needs to see you asking for help to make it easier for them to do the same?

CHAPTER FIVE

ROAD RULE 5: NO MATTER HOW ROUGH THE ROAD GETS, JUST KEEP GOING.

"To fly, we have to have resistance."

–Maya Lin, Artist, Architect, Monument Designer[22]

Introduction

We've almost made it to the end. Only one lesson left to go. And the truth is that if I had to pick only one lesson for you to learn, one lesson about confidence that would make all the difference in the world for you, it would be this one: no matter how rough your road gets, just keep going.

Do. Not. Quit.

I want you to take a moment here and think back on your life. First, I want you to think about a time when you decided there was something you really, really wanted to do. Think about whatever it was—learning to bake, taking a Spanish class, or traveling across the country. Think back to when you didn't know how you were going to do it but knew you were, and you started step-by-step, knocking out the things you needed to do—the things you needed to learn in order to make your dream, your wish, your goal happen. How did you feel? How did you feel the first time you made that fancy cake, the one you had seen in a magazine and thought, "No way, I could never make that." Or when you had a conversation with someone in Spanish for the first time and the person actually understood you. When you made it to the coastline and thought, *I never dreamed I was going to get here, but now here I am!* It was incredible, wasn't it? You felt confident, didn't you? You put the work in to do the thing you wanted to do, and it paid off.

Now think back to a time when you really, really wanted to do something, but you didn't. Maybe it was something small, like losing five pounds, finally organizing your closet, or journaling consistently. Or maybe it was something big, like going back to school, running a marathon, or starting a new hobby that you've always wanted to try, such as learning to ice skate or ballroom dance. When you think about that thing now, when you think about how you started but didn't finish—or how you never really started at all—how do you feel? If it was something you really wanted or needed to do, I'm betting you felt (and probably still feel) bad. Disappointed, frustrated, name-your-self-disparaging-adjective-here. However you felt or feel about it now, the feeling's not great. Leaves you feeling like you just found a turd in a punch bowl. Gross.

That feeling is why this section is so important. So critical. I don't want you to experience that feeling ever again. I don't want you to look back on your life and feel like you missed out on something you quit before you even started because you thought you lacked the confidence to do it. You deserve to chase your dreams, to achieve your goals, and to live your life with confidence. I want to encourage you not to quit. I want you to know that it's in the pursuit of the very things you want the most that your confidence grows exponentially. I've said it before and I'll say it again: it's in the struggle, in the pursuit of what we want, that we gain more confidence. We start off by making the choice to be confident, and we continue to gain confidence by doing what we need to do to get to where we want to go.

My friend, I want to make this as simple as possible for you to understand. You were never meant to be a quitter. In fact, I know you're not a quitter. *You're not a quitter.* If you were, you wouldn't have made it this far in the book. The world is full of quitters. You're surrounded by them every day. People who say they want to do something and who maybe even take steps to do the thing they want to do. Then when they hit an obstacle, a tough moment, or a holy-cow-I'm-going-to-crap-my-pants moment, they quit. But you're not one of them. If you want to achieve a goal, start a new career, launch a project, go back to school, learn underwater basket weaving, or whatever else floats your boat, you're going to hit obstacles. Lots of 'em. You're going to have "oh crap" moments where you feel like you aren't going to make it. You're going to have moments where you're going to try to convince yourself that you don't even want to make it, that you didn't *really* want to be a roller derby girl. But somewhere, deep down, you know you're just trying to fool yourself. You aren't a quitter. You're going to come up with a thousand reasons why you can't do whatever it is you want to do, but none of those reasons are you—they're excuses. You possess the confidence you need to do whatever you want. If you want something bad enough, you will find a way. I am confident in that.

When times get tough, you must keep going. You must keep the minivan on the road, going in the direction of your dreams. Confidence is the continued reward for those who don't quit. Let's go.

> **P.S.**
> The moment when you most want to quit, the moment
> when you feel like you've got nothing left to give,
> that moment when you feel like you just can't
> go any further, that's the moment to push hard
> and take just one more step. For in that one step, you'll
> find the confidence you didn't know you had to carry on.

School fundraisers stink

"What do you want to stop for?
You don't want to get roots; they pull you down."

–CHITA RIVERA, MUSICAL THEATER STAR[23]

I was completely confident from a very young age that a sales job was an entirely undesirable profession for someone like me. My first experience in direct sales told me so.

It was 1984, and I was in first grade at Mitchell Elementary School in Muncie, IN. Small, timid, and always skeptical of what the world might have to offer, I was given the dubious task of selling candy at a school fundraiser. I was responsible for an entire box of M&M's, Snickers, and Hershey's bars to sell for fifty cents apiece. The very success of my elementary school depended on my being able to rid myself of the contents of this box, or so I was told. I didn't care very much. I would've preferred to eat them all myself.

My mother had other ideas. Having lived through this process with my three older siblings, she was determined to make sure I learned how to sell that candy, which was partially due to her desire to see me grow and equally as likely that she didn't want to have to sell the candy herself at work. She loaded me up into the car, the white cardboard box of candy with the little yellow envelope to collect the cash clutched tightly in my tiny hands. We drove to the local college campus, Ball State University (GO BSU!), where she determined I would have great success in selling my candy to the starving students who littered the sidewalks and paths. We walked to the corner of the major intersection—I didn't know the name, only that we called it the "Blinker Light" because of the chirping sound that rang out to notify pedestrians when it was safe to cross.

There I stood in my burgundy corduroy pants, dirty shoes, and Smurfs T-shirt, ready for someone to buy my candy. My eyes scanned the street as I searched for my first customer. No one seemed to notice I was there. Terror began to creep into my heart as not a single student approached me. My mother, cautiously eyeing the situation, encouraged me to go out and ask a young man crossing the street.

"No, no, no," I said with fear in my voice.

"Yes, you will. It will be all right." Her words provided little comfort to me in my distress.

I don't want to talk to him, I thought. *I don't want to do this. I don't want him to say, 'no.'*

With a swift shove and "Go do it!" from Mom, I was launched into the intersection. I walked up to him quickly, heart pounding in my chest, hands shaking, and I muttered, "Would you like to buy some candy?" He met my eye, looked at the box and my tiny sweating hands, and said …

"No."

My tender, seven-year-old heart crumbled. I stared back at that student in shock. Then I did what any terrified, shy, and awkward kid forced into sales would do. I turned around and began screaming and crying for my mom at the top of my lungs.

That poor guy. Apparently, my outburst not only caught him off guard but garnered the attention of many of the other students also making their way to class, who then began gawking at the scene.

Panicked at my distress, the student ran over to me, grabbed a dollar from his pocket, and thrust it at me. Wiping my tears quickly, I reached in my box and grabbed the first thing on top—a bright-yellow box of Peanut M&M's. He took them and got the heck out of Dodge. With the tears drying on my cheeks, Mom drove me home; my sales day was over.

"Never again," I said to myself. I would never do sales. We bought the remaining candy in the box and returned the envelope to school.

If you were to have told me then—that little Smurfs T-shirt-wearing, shy, awkward kid—that I would find myself in a sales job, and that I would do it and love it, I would have called you a liar. And I most likely would have stomped on your foot for good measure.

Here's the deal. I think we get caught up in the idea that we need immediate, outstanding success when we're trying something new in order to feel confident. Think back to a time in your life when you started a new role, a new exercise class, or a new hobby. Were you immediately good at it? I doubt it. If you started a Zumba class, did you have all the moves down? I think not. If you were brand-new in a role as a business admin, did you know how to handle all of the incoming requests? Doubtful. How about the time you started roller skating, knitting, yoga, learning a new language? I bet you weren't immediately successful by standards set by you or by someone else. But that doesn't mean you can't feel confident about your ability to learn, to get better, and to enjoy whatever it is you've chosen to do.

I think all too often we quit things we could potentially be good or even great at, because we're unwilling to be uncomfortable with the learning process. We don't feel confident in our abilities, so we quit. We quit way too soon. Recognizing that it's our ability to choose to be confident where we are, as we are, will lead us to the next step in whatever it is we want to do.

I know this firsthand. I've come a long way since that day on campus. I didn't know it then, but a career in sales was going to be in my future whether I wanted it or not. I've had to develop confidence in myself so I could learn the processes and the strategies I needed in order to make my business profitable. I continue to work on my confidence in using sales strategies and technique in order to do what I want to do most, which is helping other people. And I get better every day.

That's something that doesn't happen if you quit. You don't get better if you quit. Sales might not be your thing, and that's OK. I want to encourage you if you're struggling with thoughts like, "I'm not good at this." Or, "I'm never going to be good at this." Or, "I'm too dumb, too old, too slow, too (fill in the blank)." Those things aren't true. You're starting out, learning, trying, testing, experimenting. Give yourself time to figure it out. If it's something you really want to do, it would be a terrible mistake for you to quit. The world needs you to keep trying. Be confident in your ability to figure it out.

P.S.
I still think school fundraisers that make kids sell stuff door-to-door are dumb. Let's just all write a check and skip the M&M's. My kid and my waistline would be grateful.

We don't poop on Hazel Dell

"People who end up as 'first' don't actually set out to be first. They set out to do something they love."

–CONDOLEEZZA RICE, SECRETARY OF STATE, CONCERT PIANIST, SOVIET UNION EXPERT[24]

Annie Lee Thompson is a former-Iowan-turned-New Yorker who moved to Indiana because of her husband's military job. Annie and I met at CrossFit where we immediately bonded over our shared love of ridiculous physical challenges and pain. She's the type of person who knows no stranger, has a smile that's contagious, and who isn't afraid to break out into spontaneous dancing if the right song comes on during a workout—or really anytime. Annie likes to dance.

We bonded after she had signed up for a half marathon and then decided she wasn't going to have enough time to train. I told her that was ridiculous, that of course she had time to train, and I committed on the spot to helping her. We trained together for six solid weeks and she finished that race. I was so stinking proud of her. She's since moved back home to Iowa, but we remain close to this day.

If you've ever spent time with someone doing something that's physically or even mentally exhausting or challenging, you know there's a special kind of bonding that takes place. You start to learn what drives another person. You learn their tells, so to speak, when they need a word of encouragement, when they need an extra push, or when they're totally sandbagging it and can do way more than what they're showing you. Annie and I, after so many miles, developed that kind of relationship. So I can tell you with one hundred percent certainty that in the case of the story I'm about to relay to you, Annie—who might have been hurting—wasn't giving me all she had. Here's what happened.

Annie was staying with me because we had a mutual friend celebrating her thirtieth birthday. As part of the weekend festivities, we planned to run together with another mutual friend, Ricki. We'd met at Ricki's house and had a stretchy five-miler on our agenda. Annie said she was nervous but was going to give it a go. I knew she'd be fine; she'd done plenty of running before, and while she might have had a lapse in her training, I had faith that all was not lost.

She did a great job right up until around mile four. She started breathing kind of heavy and murmuring about how she didn't think she was going to make it. Again, you must understand that Annie and I have run many, many miles together. I know her well. I know when she needs a break and when she needs to *suck it up* and finish the job. We were at mile four, and it was going to be a suck-it-up kind of day, whether Annie knew it or not.

We kept running, and her pace slowed a bit. She told me, "It's OK, you can go on ahead without me." That's Annie-code for, "I think I'm going to walk now, and I don't want you to see that." I told her no—I'd keep pace with her.

She slowed, and the breathing and murmuring continued.

We got to four and a half miles, and her pace got slower and her voice got louder. "Seriously, Alex, it's OK, you can go on ahead. I think I'm going to need to walk a bit. It's OK."

Nope. Nada. Not a chance. I told her we only had half a mile left, that she could do a half mile in her sleep. We were going to finish the five miles running.

She wasn't happy, but she continued—breathing and murmuring, breathing and murmuring.

When we got to the point where we only had a quarter of a mile left, Annie started begging me to stop. She was hurting. Not just hurting, mind you—at this point she was one hundred percent convinced that if she didn't stop, she was going to poop her pants, right there on Hazel Dell road.

Now that's a pretty serious concern, but again, Annie and I know each other too well. I wasn't going to let her quit—or poop, for that matter.

She kept begging me to stop. It went something like this:

- Annie: Seriously, I'm going to poop. I can't make it.
- Me: You're fine. Just keep going. We're almost there.
- (Three seconds later)
- Annie: Alex, I'm going to poop. I can't make it.
  I need to walk.
- Me: We're almost there. Just keep running.
- (Two seconds later)
- Annie: *Pleeeaaassseee,* I'm going to lose it. I can't make it!
- Me: Stop. You're fine.
- (One second later)
- Annie: Alex ... I can't ....
- (Annie starts to walk at this point.)
- Me, grabbing her elbow and yelling: ANNIE, STOP! YOU AREN'T GOING TO POOP. YOU'RE GOING TO KEEP GOING. DO YOU HEAR ME? *WE DON'T POOP ON HAZEL DELL!*
- Annie: (Gets quiet and finishes the run—with a very respectable time, I might add.)

Gross? Maybe. Harsh? Probably, and it's how we talk to each other sometimes to help push through the hard moments we don't think we'll ever be able to get through. While Annie wasn't thrilled with me in the moment, she thanked me later for the push and the pep talk/yell. (Or was it a poop talk?)

The poop isn't the point here. There's a bigger (less messy) point. The point is: never quit. Not when it's something that really matters. Not if it's something you know good and darn well you can do. Not if it's something you really want. You don't quit, and because of that, you don't let your friends quit. Whatever you've made up your mind to do, be it a physical challenge like running a race, a mental challenge like taking a certification exam, a personal challenge like losing weight, writing a book, going skydiving, quitting drinking, making your marriage work—whatever it is, you don't want to quit. And from time to time, you're going to need to surround yourself with people who can help make sure you keep at it. Especially when the going gets tough—or in keeping with our theme here—the poop is about to hit the fan. We aren't meant to do life alone. Especially when it's hard, especially when you want to quit.

Sometimes you're going to need people to have confidence in you, in your ability to get the job done, when your own confidence is hanging by a thread. You need good people in your life to give you the confidence boost or kick in the pants when you need it. If you don't have those people in your life right now, find them. Go back to lesson four and remind yourself that it's OK to ask for help, to ask for directions, to ask someone to be there for you when your confidence is wavering. I can guarantee you, if you ask and keep asking, you will find the right people to help you along the way.

Annie wanted to quit—she was afraid she was literally going to lose her poop, when really what she was losing was confidence in herself and her ability to finish the run. She needed me to push her to do better than her best, to do whatever it took to keep her going—she needed me to be confident in her. I didn't let her quit, and her confidence soared afterward. The lesson here? In life, there will be times when you are Annie and times when you are Alex. Either way, *the goal is to avoid pooping out.* The goal is to *keep going.* The goal is: don't quit.

P.S.

Annie has gone on to run many, many more races and just recently completed her fastest mile ever. Sub seven minutes. She tells me she still hears my voice whispering (or yelling) in her ear. She keeps going, no matter how bumpy the road gets.

It's not easy breaking your heart

"Being optimistic is like a muscle that gets stronger with use ...
You have to change the way you think in order to change the way you feel."
–Robin Roberts, TV Anchor, Best-Selling Author, Awareness Raiser[25]

It was going to be a stellar day. I knew it deep inside my bones. I knew it because I. Had. A. Plan. Have you ever planned for this kind of day? The kind of day where you've oh, so carefully plotted and planned each and every minute so as to maximize your time to the fullest? The kind of day when you start off fully confident that you will execute your plans with excellence and accomplish more than you thought humanly possible? The kind of day where you imagine yourself crawling into bed at exactly the time you planned, pleasantly exhausted and completely impressed with all that you had accomplished? Maybe you're like me and you imagine your husband next to you, congratulating you for being an utterly amazing woman. Yeah, that American Authors' song, "Best Day of My Life," is playing in the background.

It was going to be that kind of day. No doubt in my mind. But to say that sometimes life doesn't go as planned and that sometimes it throws you under a van, runs you over, and then backs up over you for good measure, would be an understatement. We plan, God laughs ... or so they say. It was *that* kind of day.

Despite my carefully plotted plan, it was only a quarter to nine in the morning and I was already rushing. I had decided, against my better judgment, to answer a few emails really quickly between putting the kiddo on the bus and packing my husband's lunch. (Yes, I pack his lunch because otherwise he wouldn't eat. I am *that* wife.) Why do I continue to believe the lie that I can do anything quickly and that my multitasking is a strength? I digress.

Anyway, I was rushing. I had a phone appointment that I couldn't miss, and I needed to get my butt up the stairs and get on the call in three minutes. I grabbed my coffee, shoved my laptop under my arm, and rushed up the stairs. At the time, I hadn't yet purchased office furniture. I worked from an old card table and dining room chair. My papers, various desk supplies, and random piles of junk were all crowded together on top of the table. I swept off most of it onto the floor and set up my laptop, placing my coffee cup down next to it. I had two minutes until I needed to be on my call. *Phew.*

I plopped down in my chair, took a big deep breath, and picked up my coffee mug to take a sip. To this day, I'm still not sure how it happened. Maybe it was because I had been so rushed, or maybe it was the slipperiness of the finish on the mug. It was one of those paint-your-own-pottery mugs. The kind where you go with your kids and friends and try your hand at being a pottery artist. This one I'd painted in the colors of my business logo, and it said, "This might be wine." Looking back, I think it might have been helpful— for my mental state at least—if it had been full of wine instead of coffee. Anyway, I went to take a sip, and the cup slipped right out of my hands. Right out of my hands and right onto my open laptop. All of its delicious, hot, and steamy contents poured onto the keyboard.

I can still hear my screams: "No, no, no, no!" I did the only thing that seemed rational at the time. I grabbed my computer and tipped it over directly onto my lap and the floor beneath the card table in a vain and useless attempt to get the coffee out quickly. Now I had hot coffee on my pants and feet, in addition to all over my laptop and table. *Smooth move, Alex.*

"SH#$! No! No! No! No! No! No! No!" I yelled.

I set the laptop on the floor and ran in the bathroom to grab towels, my hair dryer, Q-tips, and anything else I could think of to try to dry off my laptop. I ran back into the room and started to wipe down my computer. I had my phone with me, so I quickly searched online for "what to do when you dump coffee into your computer." Thanks, Google; it's good to know I'm definitely not the only one. I also began to fervently pray that I hadn't ruined it. I kept the laptop open, typing and hitting buttons to make sure it worked, and for a while it did. Then, slowly, a few of the keys stopped, the mouse died, and then with a final gasp, the screen went black.

SH#$. I was supposed to be on a call. I stopped and picked up my phone. I took a deep breath and thought, *OK, I can do this. I know Jen. I'll just tell her what happened, and we'll do the call and then I'll figure this out.* I called Jen and as soon as she picked up, I phone-vomited to her what had happened. Thankfully, she said the magic words I needed to hear in that moment.

"Uh, do you want to go ahead and take care of your computer and call me back later?"

Yes, yes, I do.

I hung up and looked at the web pages I'd pulled up on my phone about coffee and laptops. There were a thousand and one ways the internet suggested I handle this, including taking it apart myself and drying out the pieces individually. *Uh, no, thank you.* I briefly considered filling my bathtub with rice and putting my laptop in it, but a.) I didn't have enough rice to fill a garden tub, and b.) I knew no matter what I tried, I wasn't going to be able to fix this *myself*.

So I changed out of my coffee-stained jeans, packed up my soggy laptop, and I headed off to Best Buy. I'd purchased it there and knew I'd gotten some sort of protection plan, so I figured if anyone could help me, it was them. Wish I'd checked the clock before I left because it was only a quarter to ten when I got there. The store wasn't open yet. Thank goodness I had my phone and USB cord so I could numb the pain of the morning's events with Facebook scrolling. At ten o'clock, I was the first person in the door. I went straight to the Geek Squad desk and asked the friendly Geek (their term, not mine) at the counter if he could help me. I explained that I'd dumped an entire cup of coffee on my laptop and asked if they could fix that. He tried to mask the horror on his face, but I could see it. He said, "Uh, well, I'd recommend you go straight to the Apple store for something like that. I mean, it's probably trashed, and you'll have to get a new one."

Not helpful. Not helpful at all. I looked at him and muttered something to the effect of going to the Apple store is like visiting the Seventh Circle of Hell for me, but if that was my only option, I would do just that, and I walked right back out of the store. I hopped in the van and looked up the number for the Apple store. I called and was informed by the friendly Apple robot that I'd have to put in a request for a time and then wait for a call. *Seriously?* I thought. OK, I'll put in my request and start heading that way. The closest Apple store is thirty minutes away from my house.

I drove over, then ended up sitting in the parking lot and waiting for the call for over an hour. Why I chose to do that, I can't tell you. I was shaken up, and I just wanted to know that I could get my laptop fixed. When Apple finally called and the automated voice gave me permission to enter the store, I went in and sat on the weird little blocks designated for us poor souls with broken technology, waiting for an assistant to come find me.

Sitting there, waiting for help to come, I felt the weight of what had happened, and my fear started to sink in. I started to fight back tears. I was brand new in my business—I mean, for goodness' sake, I didn't even have a desk yet. I had worked so hard to create what I had: plans, outlines, spreadsheets, contact lists. My dreams in written form. Ideal clients fleshed out in words. Ideas just beginning to take shape. I had all of it on my laptop. My laptop that was still damp in my hands because of the coffee. My laptop that sat at the heart of my business, and was now, in all likelihood, not going to be fixed. At least not in the way I really needed it to be. I needed it *all* back. Almost everything I had was on there, and it wasn't saved to the cloud, or anywhere else for that matter. I had lost all my work. It was soul-crushing to think about starting it all over again. How on Earth was I going to get it all back? What on Earth was I going to do?

My eyes were blurry as I looked at all the stressed out faces around me. People sitting alone on their weird little blocks. Devices clutched in their hands and pained expressions on their faces. I wondered how many of them had just lost what was important to them on their devices. I wondered how many of them had backups saved. I wondered how many of them felt as dumb and as sad as I did in that moment. Seeing how stressed they looked made me wonder if I looked equally as pained as they did. I imagine I probably looked worse, sitting there with a coffee-stained laptop, messy bun, and now tear-streaked face.

The song "Not Easy" by Alex Da Kid came on over the speakers. It's one of those bittersweet and mildly upbeat love songs, and while the lyrics don't necessarily reflect the situation exactly, it's just one of *those* songs. You know what I mean, the kind you play when you're feeling down, but it's got a sort of happy beat, so it doesn't throw you into a bout of ugly crying. The refrain is: "It's not easy," which at that moment summarized how I felt about life.

I started thinking about how dependent we are on our tech gadgets and computers. How much we freak out when something goes wrong with them. How something like a cup of coffee, spilled by accident, threatens to ruin our day, our week, our month. How easily we slip into the idea that something like a coffee-soaked computer could ruin a life. How many times have you had something happen in your day that seems like a *complete disaster*, but really you know it isn't? A fender bender that messed up your new car, the water heater going out, a fight with your spouse, your kid flunking a math test.

How many times have you thought, *This ruins everything? I'm just going to quit.* I've had that thought way more times than I care to count, and I had it for sure that day. I was sure I had lost all my stuff. I was going to have to start over at square one. I wanted to quit.

As I sat there on my cube, listening to the music, I thought, *All is not lost. I haven't lost anything I can't get back. So I lost some files. Yup, I'm going to have to recreate a ton of stuff. I'm going to have to make some changes as to how I save my stuff from here on out. There's no doubt. And ... I don't want to be this stressed out over a computer. Everyone I care about is OK. Everything I've done, made, created can be created again. Maybe some of it will be better for it. I have people around me that will help. What I'm doing is important—it's important not to quit. I can't let a cup of friggin' coffee stop me from doing what I need to do, for goodness' sake.*

I started swaying, smiling, and making eye contact with every pained face I could because *I feel better when I smile*, and I bet they (and you) do too. If I looked like a nut to someone, I didn't care. I knew that if I put my mind to it, I could figure this out. I was confident in that, if nothing else. It's hard not to give up when we're in the moment, when we're stressed and worried and afraid. But there is always a way to keep moving forward—we just have to look for it. And I knew there were many more important things in life than computers.

By the time the Apple guy got to me, I was ready to hear about the damage. I made him laugh, telling him that he'd be cursing me later because I made sure the coffee touched every single part of the computer. Every part. Ultimately, they were able to salvage the outer shell and nothing else. It was a loss for sure, but not a complete loss.

It's hard, my friend, to keep going in the face of challenges. It's hard to keep going when it feels like nothing is going your way and no one is on your side. It's hard when you feel like your struggles are never going to end. But I promise you this: if you try, you *can* and you *will* find a way to keep moving forward. Whatever you have gone through or are going through that's a struggle, it's something that you can and will get through. I promise if you just focus on doing the next right thing, taking the next small step, that tiny inch forward, you'll find the road that lies ahead is easier to navigate. You'll find you can come back from that bump, pothole, or sinkhole that's trying to swallow you up, and you'll be a smarter, stronger, and more confident person than you were before. *Keep moving forward.*

P.S.
The use of cups without lids is now banned within fifteen feet of me and my computer. I've also managed to learn how to save stuff to the cloud. I'm confident that the next time disaster strikes, I'll be better prepared.

Finish what you've started

"Forward is not a straight line. It's much more exciting, difficult, gnarly, and uncharted than that."

–JENI BRITTON BAUER, ARTISAN ICE CREAM MAKER,
B-CORP FOUNDER, AMATEUR PERFUMER[26]

Seventeen years ago, I walked my first half marathon. A few friends of mine from work were walking it, and they invited me to come. I said yes, having zero idea what I was getting into. I hadn't been a high school athlete, and I didn't exercise. I was significantly overweight, a closet smoker, and thought Fruity Pebbles were an OK choice for breakfast, lunch, and dessert. Truth be told, I still think Fruity Pebbles make an excellent choice for an anytime treat, but that's a whole other subject. I signed up to walk that half marathon, and I was going to do it, by golly. (Who says "by golly" anymore? I am, indeed, turning into my mother. *Sigh.*)

Anyway, I wasn't about to make a fool of myself in front of my friends, so despite being tired after mile one, questioning my sanity after mile six, and praying for my own demise after mile ten, I finished that darn half marathon. It took me nearly four hours. If you're someone who likes to count, that equates to roughly an eighteen-minute mile. I most definitely didn't break any records that day. The fact that I didn't break my foot or a leg or some other body part is a miracle. Once I finished, I spent the rest of the day alternating between soaking in a hot bath and lying on the couch, wondering what the heck I had been thinking and vowing to never, ever do something like that again.

Never say never. Somewhere along that thirteen-mile walk, I'd found confidence I hadn't known I had. Confidence to finish what I started. Confidence to do something many people won't do. A challenge of both my mental and physical strength. And if I'd had confidence enough to do it once, it made me wonder if I could do it again. What would happen if next time, I really put some effort into a race and gave it my best? What could I do?

Turns out, I can do a lot. Since that first, slow walk, I've gone on to run over thirty half marathons, five full marathons, and countless 5Ks. And I'm proud, very proud to say I've finished every race I've ever signed up for. Every race. Races that were so hot I could barely breathe and I thought for sure I was going to die of dehydration. Races where my feet sank into the snow and I thought for sure I was going to get frostbite and lose my toes. There was the marathon where I twinged my knee on mile fifteen, and I called my husband on my flip phone and cried. He said he'd come and get me right then, and I told him to wait because I wanted to see if I could limp through to mile sixteen.

And I did. I limped through sixteen, seventeen, and all the way through until I crossed the finish line. There were times when I ran sick and when I ran tired. I even ran when I had to poop so bad I thought I'd explode, but I didn't. That's why I screamed at Annie on Hazel Dell—I knew if I'd made it through a run poop-free, she could too. I've run alone, and I've run with groups of friends. I've run scared that I wouldn't finish, but every time—*every time*—I've dug deep and found the confidence I know exists within me, and I've chosen to use it. I've always chosen to believe that I could, even when it seemed impossible, and, as a result, my confidence has grown with each race I've completed.

To this day, I finish my races not because I'm an elite athlete, genetically superior, or somehow gifted. I finish because I'm unwilling to quit. I haven't won any awards, I've never broken any records, nor have I ever finished first. I'm not telling you this because I'm some sort of running hero. There's nothing exceptional about my running from an athletic standpoint. What is exceptional, though, is that I've found the confidence each and every time not to quit, and, by doing so, I've been able to accumulate more confidence with each mile, each race, and each goal I've set.

If I had quit at any point on the tough days, during the tough races, or when I thought I couldn't go any farther, I wouldn't be the person I am today. Chances are, if I hadn't dug deep to find the confidence that I know exists within me, that exists within all of us, I wouldn't have lost the weight, quit smoking, started eating healthy, and started making all sorts of other choices a confident woman makes. Choices like asking for what I want, having a tough conversation, saying no when I don't want to do something, taking care of myself first, resting …. I could go on and on, but I think you catch my drift. When you decide to keep going even when you want to quit, when you choose to be confident about your ability to finish what you've started, the ripple effect of confidence takes hold on your entire life.

Too many people are willing to give up on their dreams, pursuits, or goals because they don't feel they have what it takes to accomplish their goals or to make their own dreams come true. Too many people are willing to quit before they've even started down the road of pursuing what they want, when they want it. Too many people quit too soon because they hit a bump in the road, get pulled over for speeding, or get a flat tire, and they don't keep going because they lack the confidence to know how to deal with their problems.

Too many people don't feel confident they can pursue what they want at "the right time" or "in the right way." They quit because they don't think they have what it takes. Because it doesn't come naturally, or easy, or fast enough. They quit because they're tired or scared or not seeing the progress they want the moment they want it. They don't feel like they deserve to have what they really want. They're unwilling to finish what they've started because it takes work. So they make excuses for why they can't do something, and they live out those excuses.

Hear me out: I'm not talking about quitting something that is bad for you. There are plenty of things you can and should quit doing—like smoking, eating too much crappy food, drinking too much, gossiping, telling little white lies, making excuses, and allowing toxic people into your life. Those are things we can and must quit doing for sure. I'm talking about quitting important things. The thing you've always wanted to do, like going back to school, starting a new business, trying a new sport, creating art, recording a podcast, volunteering for an organization, or writing a book.

I know I've talked a lot about running, and running may or may not be your thing. But I bet there's something you've signed up for, something you said you wanted to do and haven't yet accomplished. You've started the thing, and right now it's uncomfortable, scary, or you just plain stink at it. Maybe it hurts mentally or physically and you're feeling defeated. And you want to give up, you're making excuses in your head or out loud, and you're killing your confidence by doing so. You want to quit. Or maybe you've only managed to think about the thing you want to do so badly, but you've convinced yourself of all the reasons why you can't, which is essentially quitting before you ever get started.

My friend, if you take nothing else away from this book— nothing else—please take this away: DO. NOT. QUIT. There is no single bigger confidence killer than giving up on your goal, on your dream.

Of course, there will be days, many days, where you want more than anything to give up and walk away because you can't see the finish line. There will be days, minutes, hours where you'll tell yourself you didn't really want whatever it is you wanted, and you'll work hard to convince yourself to quit. But it's in these moments you need to remember this lesson the most: You must not quit. You're going to have to dig deep. You're going to have to push hard. You'll probably fall down, make a ton of mistakes, and you're going to have to face many challenges and things that don't go according to plan. That's where you get to build your confidence muscles over and over and over again. Until you've completed the race, you've written the story, you've opened the business, you've gotten the job, you've done the thing you want to do. And when you've finished what you've started on that particular journey, when you've found your confidence in the hard work on the road to whatever is you want, that's when you get to start a new journey and do it all over again. And this time you'll be stronger, smarter, and more confident than before.

P.S.
Don't quit.
I believe in you.

Remember: No matter how rough the road gets, just keep going.

ANSWER THE FOLLOWING QUESTIONS

1. What are you thinking about quitting today, and why? Is there something you should quit because it's not working for you anymore?

2. How do you know the difference between something you want to quit because it's dragging you down, and something you want to quit because it feels "too hard"?

3. How will you feel if you choose not to quit that thing that's bringing you out of your comfort zone?

4. How will your confidence improve if you choose to keep working, even though it might feel good to quit in the moment?

5. How will your life improve if you choose not to quit?

CONCLUSION

"The road doesn't end here."

–ME, MINIVAN MOM, CHEETOS LOVER, AUTHOR

I didn't set out to write a book. That was never part of the plan. However, here I am at the end, and I am happy. Relieved, excited, and a little bit tired too. I'm not a millionaire mogul—I'm a minivan-driving mom who gets up every day and lives out the road rules I've shared with you in this book. In order to get this unexpected project done, I had to be confident that I would and *could* get it done. I had to choose to be confident that I could write something, anything, when I sat down in front of my computer. I had to choose to keep my eyes on the road in front of me, ignoring other people—my friends who have written books, celebrity authors, and every other author I came across while I wrote this.

I've had to own every single awkward variation of this book. (Oh Lord, have mercy, if you could only see where this started—as a book called *The Leadership Presence Myth ... sigh ...* we all start somewhere.) I had to ask for all kinds of help. There have been countless people who listened to me, who read rough drafts, and who helped me with the process of getting this book to its completed form.

And last but not least, I didn't quit. Though I definitely wanted to. Not when it got hard (which it did—a lot). Not when I wanted to believe that no one would read this, not even my friends. Not when I wanted to believe that the world didn't need one more self-help book, because it did—it needed mine. I didn't quit. And now, it's done. I don't know whether this book will be a success or not, but I have WRITTEN A BOOK. Confidence for the WIN! And as an added bonus, I'll be more confident in the process next time around.

The truth is, you'll use my advice, use these road rules in confidence, in your own way, on your own terms, and that's the way it's supposed to be. My hope is that these rules serve as a guide to help you be confident in who you are, exactly as you are, right now in this moment, no matter what is going on around you. I meant it when I said I see you, striving so hard to be one in a million that you forget you already are. Be confident in that truth. Take these rules and make them your own. The confidence that will follow will change your life.

OK, we've come to a good stopping place on our journey. I hope I've lived up to the promise I made to you at the beginning of this book: that we'd laugh, we'd cry, and we'd spend moments of silence together, just being ourselves. I hope you walk away from this trip we've taken together, remembering these rules and knowing that, like a good minivan-driving mom does, I'm cheering you on every single day. I am confident in you.

And while this particular trip has come to an end, we aren't finished yet. Confidence isn't a destination, it's a process—a constant journey you and I are both on. As we drive together through life, we'll learn more, we'll share more, and we'll become even more confident in who we are and in each other. This is the first of what I hope to be many books I write for you as we travel along the road of life together. The road doesn't end here. My friend, I am so grateful you chose to spend part of your journey with me. Until the next trip.

All my love,

Alex

AFTERWORD

ONE LAST STOP

"I will not follow where the path may lead, but I will go where there is no path, and I will leave a trail."
—MURIEL STRODE, AUTHOR, POET, TRAILBLAZER[27]

There's always one more stop before we get to where we're going.

Before I started writing *Minivan Mogul*, I had no idea about how the process of editing a book comes to pass. In my mind, you hand your book over to an editor, the editor reads through it and fixes all your spelling and grammar mistakes, and you call it done. I figured editors were like a sort of human spell-check, with super-speedy eyes and an amazing talent for recalling every grammar rule taught in school.

I was wrong. Dead wrong.

Turns out, there's all kinds of editing involved in the book editing process, from the developmental kind where your editor helps you flesh out the ideas of your book thoroughly, to line edits to make sure your language is clear and concise, to copyediting where the editor combs through your book for all sorts of other errors you can think of. And after all of those rounds are complete, then, and only then, does your book get proofread to make sure nothing has been missed.

To summarize, editors do a whole lot more than I ever gave them credit for before this process (I apologize, Karli, Amy, and Monika).

Though I became more educated while the editing process went along, I was still unprepared for what I was going to see when Karli returned my first round of line edits. It was like being in second grade again, having written, what in my mind, was my most brilliant masterpiece, only to have it returned by the teacher covered in red pen marks. Like in *A Christmas Story* when Ralphie gets his Red Ryder BB gun essay back from the teacher and it's got a big red C+ on it ... that was me.

The truth is, I opened up my newly-edited version of *Minivan Mogul*, took one look at all the red marks on the page (page one, mind you ... page one. I didn't even bother to scroll to the other pages,) and I slammed my computer shut. I slammed it shut, and I didn't look at my book again for almost three weeks. I did my best not to even think about it.

Those red marks had sent me into a complete tailspin for two reasons. The first reason, hysterically enough, is that I had NO IDEA how to get the red marks to go away in Microsoft Word. I looked at all that red and thought, "How on Earth am I going to fix all of that? It will take me years, and I'm already not great at the whole spelling/grammar thing. WHAT HAVE YOU DONE TO ME, KARLI?"

You see, I'd never used the editing feature of Word, and so I didn't realize all I had to do was click the "Accept" button to make the changes. Which is hilarious—now. *Now* it's hilarious. At the time, it was paralyzing.

The other reason I spun out was because it's one thing to be writing a book and a completely different thing to *have written* a book. Let me explain. When you're writing a book, everyone thinks that's cool. People might say, "Oh, man, you're writing a book, that's so cool," or "What a challenge to undertake!" or "Man, I could never write a book. I can't wait to see yours." For a verbal affirmation junkie like me, this kind of stuff never gets old. It *is* cool to be writing a book. But it's scary as you-know-what to *have* written a book.

I'm terrified of you seeing it.

I'm a minivan-driving mom from the Midwest. I have like thirteen followers on Instagram. I barely know how to use Word. And for goodness' sake, why even write a book when Brené Brown exists? (Gosh, I love her.)

You see, *writing* a book is safe. There's no real risk of judgment, rejection, or public shaming. I don't have to read negative comments or see data around sales. I don't have to wonder if people are telling me it's good just to spare my feelings. I'm tucked up in my cozy chair in my fuzzy robe with a cup of coffee, typing away to you like we're old friends. I don't have to worry about things like social media or Oprah or whatever. I'm safely writing a book that no one can judge but me.

But when the line edits came back, they signaled to me that the book was on its way to being done. And if it's done, that means it goes out into the world. And what happens if it goes out into the world and …

- … only my mom buys copies of it so I don't feel bad about myself?
- … no one buys it?
- … they buy it and hate it?
- … it gets all sorts of awful comments on Amazon?
- … it gets NO comments on Amazon?
- … it fails?

Looking back, I slammed my laptop closed not because the red marks were unmanageable, but because the idea of being one step closer to having the book done scared me. A lot.

Three weeks passed before Karli and I hopped on the phone to talk through the line edits. I explained that I had no idea how to make the red marks go away, we had a great laugh, and she walked me through how to click a button. Turns out, I wasn't going to have to make all the edits manually after all. And with every click, my book was getting better and closer to being out in the world.

And that made me think: Wouldn't it be wonderful if we had an "Accept" button? A button we could click for ourselves that would help us accept the parts of us that need improvement, or more importantly, one that would bolster us to accept the things about ourselves that make us so special and so wonderful?

You see, every time I clicked the "Accept" button for this book, I was fixing technical errors that would get in the way of you understanding and enjoying what I had to say. And I was accepting that this book was not only going to be published, but that it would be enjoyed by someone.

Someone like you. (Because, goodness knows, if you've made it this far and you're not my mom or an editor, you have enjoyed this book.)

By clicking the "Accept" button, I was acknowledging that this book was an accurate representation of me. Not perfect, not flawless, but *real*. Quirky, funny, insightful, sometimes irreverent, sarcastic, and in need of directional help more often than I care to admit. A minivan-driving mom who, despite her battles with insecurity, technology, and self-doubt, started her own successful consulting business, is raising a crazy-confident teenager, became a TEDx speaker, and is now an author.

I had to accept all of those things in order for this book to see the light of day.

Click.

My friend, the next time you find yourself in a spot where you're scared of what "the world" will think, when you're terrified about being judged, when all you want to do is curl up in your cozy chair and *not* face the world ... I want you to think of your "Accept" button.

I want you to see it in your mind's eye.

I want you to hover your finger over it.

Then with all of your might, press down.

Click.

ENDNOTES

1 Bold & Untold by MAKERS, profile of Judaline Cassidy. 2018. "Construction Was Clogged With Sexism—Until She Fought For More Women In The Pipeline." Facebook, 12 September, 2018. https://www.facebook.com/watch/?v=873155299521828.

2 Danielle Young, "6 Ava DuVernay Quotes to Reaffirm Your #BlackGirlMagic," *Essence* (Essence Communications, July 2, 2016), https://www.essence.com/lifestyle/ava-duvernay-essence-empower-experience-speech/.

3 Anna Moeslein, "Reese Witherspoon's Moving Speech at Glamour's 2015 Women of the Year Awards: 'Like Elle Woods, I Do Not Like to Be Underestimated.'," Glamour (Condé Nast, November 10, 2015), https://www.glamour.com/story/reese-witherspoon-women-of-the-year-speech.

4 Coretta Scott King, foreword to *Strength to Love* (Minneapolis: Fortress Press, 2010).

5 Eunice Kennedy Shriver, "Minerva Awards Acceptance Speech," The Women's Conference, (October 23, 2007), YouTube. https://www.youtube.com/watch?=UJpcXHYX4v4.

6 "Effusive," in Lexico (Oxford University), accessed February 1, 2020, https://www.lexico.com/en/definition/effusive.

7 Joseph Keefe, "Five Minutes with Captain Kate McCue," *Maritime Professional*, accessed February 22, 2020, https://www.maritimeprofessional.com/magazine/story/201509/minutes-captain-mccue-499370.

8   "Female Racer's Lessons from Life in the Fast Lane." Interview of Milka Duno by Felicia Taylor. *CNN International Edition,* Turner Broadcasting System, Inc. June 15, 2012. https://edition.cnn.com/2012/06/15/living/milka-duno-racecar-driver/index.html.

9   Christina Austin, "Venus Williams' Best Business Advice? Say 'No' with a Smile," *Fortune* (Fortune Media IP Limited, September 7, 2017), https://fortune.com/2017/09/07/us-open-2017-venus-williams-business-advice/.

10 Natalie Franke, as quoted in *Grit & Grace: Uncommon Wisdom for Inspiring Leaders, Designed to Make You Think* (Lexington, Kentucky: Rock Point, The Quarto Group, 2018).

11 Jeff Beer, "How Patagonia Grows Every Time It Amplifies Its Social Mission," *Fast Company,* February 21, 2018, https://www.fastcompany.com/40525452/how-patagonia-grows-every-time-it-amplifies-its-social-mission.

12 Danielle Weisberg and Carly Zakin, "Billy, Don't Be a Hero: Our Top Meltdowns," *The Skimm Blog* (Medium, November 16, 2017), https://blog.theskimm.com/billy-dont-be-a-hero-our-top-meltdowns-45b55cdea484.

13 Lisa Immordino Vreeland, "Diana Vreeland Profile," Harper's Bazaar, August 26, 2011, https://www.harpersbazaar.com/culture/features/a775/diana-vreeland-bazaar-years-0911.

14 Tina Essmaker, "Dana Tanamachi: Designer/Illustrator/Typographer," *The Great Discontent,* March 20, 2012.

15 "Tenley Albright, M.D., Interview," Academy of Achievement, American Academy of Achievement, updated May 3, 2019, https://achievement.org/achiever/tenley-albright-m-d/#interview.

16 Maria Popova, "Happy Birthday, Brain Pickings: 7 Things I Learned in 7 Years of Reading, Writing, and Living," *Brain Pickings* (blog), October 23, 2013, https://www.brainpickings.org/2013/10/23/7-lessons-from-7-years.

17 Fannie Merritt Farmer, *The 1896 Boston Cooking-School Cookbook,* facsimile ed. (1896; repr., New York: Gramercy Publishing Company, 1997).

18 "Alice Walker Calls God 'Mama,'" Interview, beliefnet, February 2007, accessed April 24, 2020, http://www.beliefnet.com/wellness/2007/02alice-walker-calls-god-mama.aspx.

19 Kelly Holmes, *Just Go for It!* (Carlsbad, California: Hay House Publishers, 2011).

20 Amanda Palmer, *The Art of Asking: How I Learned to Stop Worrying and Let People Help,* reprint ed. (2014, repr., New York: Grand Central Publishing, 2015).

21 "63 Fascinating Google Stats," Seotribunal.com, September 26, 2018, accessed February 15, 2020.

22 Maya Lin, as quoted in *Grit & Grace: Uncommon Wisdom for Inspiring Leaders, Designed to Make You Think* (Lexington, Kentucky: Rock Point, The Quarto Group, 2018).

23 Margaret Gray, "Q&A: Chita Rivera on Touring, and Staying Political, at Age 84," *LA Times,* February 6, 2017.

24 Alana Glass, "NFL Women's Summit: Condoleezza Rice Talks Diversity and Inclusion in Sports," *Forbes,* February 5, 2016, https://www.forbes.com/sites/alanaglass/2016/02/05/nfl-womens-summit-condoleezza-rice-talks-diversity-and-inclusion-in-sports/#1321555b65a6.

25 Robin Roberts and Veronica Chambers, *Everybody's Got Something,* (New York: Grand Central Publishing, 2014).

26 Jeni Britton Bauer, "Let's go FORWARD AMERICA," *Jeni's* (blog), January 20, 2017, https//jenis.com/blog/lets-go-forward-america.

27 Muriel Strode, "Wind-Wafted Wild Flowers," *The Open Court,* Vol. 17, No. 8, August, 1903.

BIBLIOGRAPHY

Academy of Achievement. "Tenley Albright, M.D., Interview." American Academy of Achievement. Updated May 3, 2019, https://achievement.org/achiever/tenley-albright-md/#interview.

Austin, Christina. "Venus Williams' Best Business Advice? Say 'No' with a Smile." *Fortune*. Fortune Media IP Limited, September 7, 2017. https://fortune.com/2017/09/07/us-open-2017-venus-williams-business-advice/.

Beer, Jeff. "How Patagonia Grows Every Time It Amplifies Its Social Mission." *Fast Company*, February 21, 2018. https://www.fastcompany.com/40525452/how-patagonia-grows-every-time-it-amplifies-its-social-mission.

Beliefnet. "Alice Walker Calls God 'Mama.'" Interview. February 2007. Accessed April 24, 2020. http://www.beliefnet.com/wellness/2007/02alice-walker-calls-god-mama.aspx.

Bauer, Jeni Britton. *Let's go FORWARD AMERICA* (blog). https//jenis.com/blog/lets-go-forward-america.

"Construction Was Clogged With Sexism—Until She Fought For More Women In The Pipeline." Bold & Untold by MAKERS, profile of Judaline Cassidy. Facebook, 12 September, 2018. https://www.facebook.com/watch/?v=873155299521828

"Effusive." In *Lexico*. Oxford University. Accessed February 1, 2020. https://www.lexico.com/en/definition/effusive.

Farmer, Fannie Merritt. *The 1896 Boston Cooking-School Cookbook*. 1896. Facsimile of the first edition. New York: Gramercy Publishing Company, 1997.

"Female Racer's Lessons from Life in the Fast Lane." Interview of Milka Duno by Felicia Taylor. *CNN International Edition*, Turner Broadcasting System, Inc. June 15, 2012. https://edition.cnn.com/2012/06/15/living/milka-duno-racecar-driver/index.html.

Glass, Alana. "NFL Women's Summit: Condoleezza Rice Talks Diversity and Inclusion in Sports." *Forbes*. February 5, 2016. https://www.forbes.com/sites/alanaglass/2016/02/05/nfl-womens-summit-condoleezza-rice-talks-diversity-and-inclusion-in-sports/#1321555b65a6.

Gray, Margaret. "Q&A: Chita Rivera on Touring, and Staying Political, at Age 84." *LA Times*. February 6, 2017.

Grit & Grace: Uncommon Wisdom for Inspiring Leaders, Designed to Make You Think. Lexington, Kentucky: Rock Point, 2018.

Holmes, Kelly. *Just Go for It!* Carlsbad, California: Hay House Publishers, 2011.

Keefe, Joseph. "Five Minutes with Captain Kate McCue." *Maritime Professional*. Accessed February 22, 2020. https://www.maritimeprofessional.com/magazine/story/201509/minutes-captain-mccue-499370.

King Jr., Martin Luther. *Strength to Love*. With foreword by Coretta Scott King. Minneapolis: Fortress Press, 2010.

Lisa Immordino Vreeland, "Diana Vreeland Profile," *Harper's Bazaar*, August 26, 2011, https://www.harpersbazaar.com/culture/features/a775/diana-vreeland-bazaar-years-0911.

Moeslein, Anna. "Reese Witherspoon's Moving Speech at Glamour's 2015 Women of the Year Awards: 'Like Elle Woods, I Do Not Like to Be Underestimated'." Glamour. Condé Nast, November 10, 2015. https://www.glamour.com/story/reese-witherspoon-women-of-the-year-speech.

Palmer, Amanda. *The Art of Asking: How I Learned to Stop Worrying and Let People Help*. 2014. Reprint edition. New York: Grand Central Publishing, 2015.

Popova, Maria. *Brain Pickings* (blog). https://www.brainpickings.org.

Roberts, Robin and Veronica Chambers. *Everybody's Got Something*. New York: Grand Central Publishing, 2014.

Shriver, Eunice Kennedy. "Minerva Awards Acceptance Speech," The Women's Conference, October 23, 2007, YouTube. https://www.youtube.com/watch?=UJpcXHYX4v4.

Strode, Muriel. "Wind-Wafted Wild Flowers." *The Open Court,* August, 1903.

Tina Essmaker, "Dana Tanamachi: Designer/Illustrator/Typographer," *The Great Discontent,* March 20, 2012.

Weisberg, Danielle, and Carly Zakin. "Billy, Don't Be a Hero: Our Top Meltdowns." *The Skimm Blog.* Medium, November 16, 2017. https://blog. theskimm.com/billy-dont-be-a-hero-our-top-meltdowns-45b55cdea484.

Young, Danielle. "6 Ava DuVernay Quotes to Reaffirm Your #BlackGirlMagic." *Essence.* Essence Communications, July 2, 2016. https://www.essence.com/ lifestyle/ava-duvernay-essence-empower-experience-speech/

CPSIA information can be obtained
at www.ICGtesting.com
Printed in the USA
FSHW010801140920
73401FS